Hey Stewart!

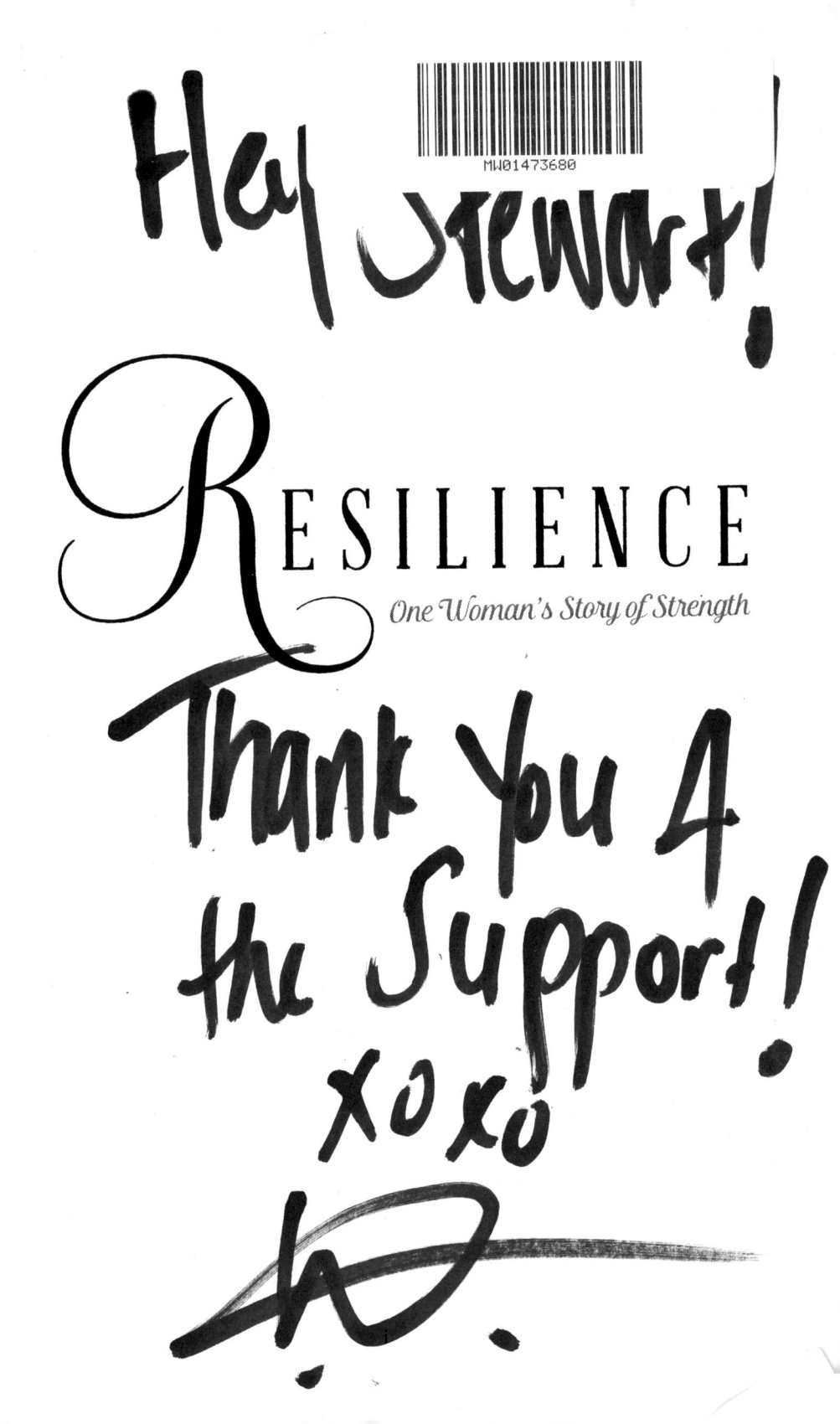

RESILIENCE
One Woman's Story of Strength

Thank you 4 the Support!
xoxo

Hey Stewart!

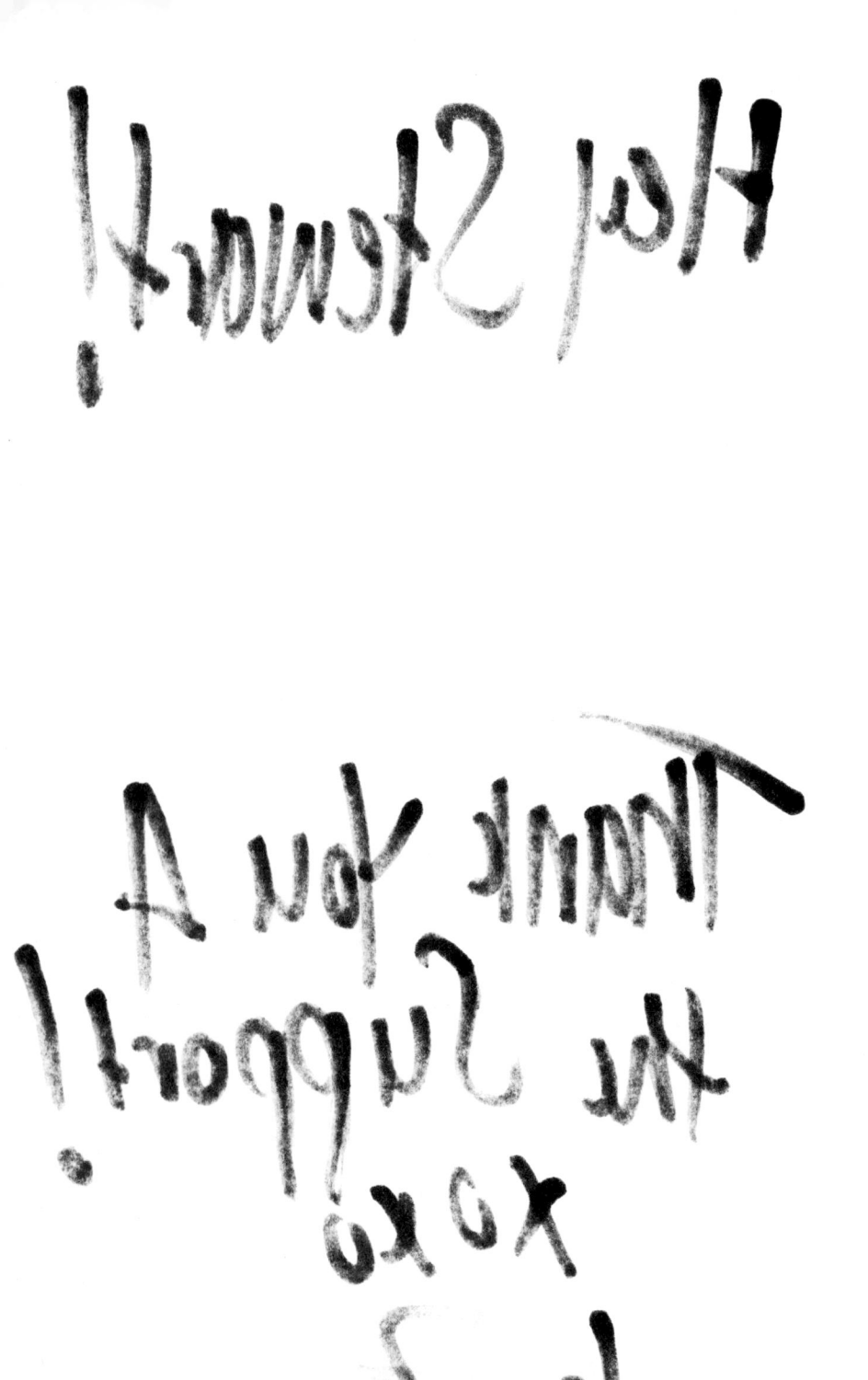

Thank you 4
the Support!
xoxo

RESILIENCE
One Woman's Story of Strength

Tasheka Mason

CONCLUSIO
HOUSE PUBLISHING

Copyright © 2016 by Tasheka Mason

All rights reserved. This book or any portion thereof may not be reproduced or used in any manner whatsoever without the express written permission of the publisher except for the use of brief quotations in a book review.

"Resilience: One Woman's Story of Strength"

Printed in Canada
First Printing, 2016

ISBN 978-0-9949204-6-1

Published by:
Conclusio House Publishing
503-7700 Hurontario Street
Suite 209
Brampton, ON
L6Y 4M3

www.conclusiohouse.com

Disclaimer: Except for those who have given their expressed permission, all names and identifiable characteristics have been changed to protect the true identities of individuals mentioned in this book.

To my queen, Fredericka Thompson. Thank you!

"Thank you, mama, for the nine months you carried me through
All those pain and suffering,
No one knows the pressure you bare, a just only you,
Give you all my love, oh yea.
Thank you, mama, for the nine months you carried me through,
All those pain and suffering,
No one knows the pressure you bare, a just only you,
This is my words and my uttering,
Mama, I would never let you down,
I'll never go away, I'll always be around.
You know why you do it, such love that you found,
I'm always gonna let you wear that crown,
Through the roughest of times you maintain your calm,
Jah was your only help while sheltering me from the storm,
And when it's cold, you wrap me in a towel so warm
Oh Ma, oh Ma, I'm so glad I was born."

- Sizzla, Thank you, Mama

Acknowledgements

After reading a book like *Dear Dad* by Kymani Marley about four or five times, I thought to myself, Why am I scared to write my own story? The book was so inspiring. The way he wrote his story was so bold and without fear of what others may think that it really touched me. I appreciated that experience, Kymani.

First of all, I would like to thank God for His grace and mercies that brought me through all my triumphs and challenges in life. Without you, Lord, this book would never be. Thank you for answering my prayers and for taking me through the process and for providing me with the resources needed to release this book.

Thanks to Cassava Piece, Kingston, Jamaica that raised me throughout my early years.

Speaking of Jamaica, special thanks to my big sister, Tammy Purge, who gave up her life to take care of me, tirelessly, while my mother worked way too hard to support us. Tammy, a.k.a. 'Mummy', you were my very first believer before anyone else. You believed in me and saw my potential before I even knew I had any. To this day, you remain so humble, yet so ambitious, in your own right. I don't think I can ever repay you for the unconditional love you've given me over the years.

Thank you, Jemelia, a.k.a. 'My right hand', and family for taking me in like your own, for loving and caring for me when I needed you the most. Thank you for your contributions—financially, emotionally, and spiritually—to the process of publishing this book. Most of all, thank you for believing in me.

Thank you to Beno, a.k.a. Christie, for being a great stepmother who tried to strengthen the relationship between my father and me.

A very special thank you to Arsema Berhane. I don't think I've ever had a manager who believed in me as much as you did. You supported my passion and dreams as an entrepreneur so much that you allowed me the flexibility, during work hours, to book speaking engagements and to work on my book. I started working with you when I had a book I needed to publish, and you had no questions about the success of this book, you just said, "We need to get your book published. And whatever I can do to help, do not hesitate to let me know, sis." I thank God for our connection. As I always tell you, you are my 'big sister angel.' You will never know how much I appreciate and love you for having everlasting faith in me. I don't know another manager as awesome as you. Speaking of Arsema, thanks to her lovely husband, Danavan Samuels, for being a mentor and big brother who always pushes me to the top. Thank you for always challenging my way of thinking so that I can reach my full potential. Thank you for your input when I was choosing the name for this book; as you can see, it meant a lot. Thanks especially to you both for your support with my professional development as a Social Service Worker.

Thank you to my pastor, Dr. William Lee, for believing in and supporting me and this book, and for your continuous pouring into me as a child of God.

Thank you to my father, Alton Mason, for taking me to Canada. A lot of fathers have not done what you did after leaving their home country, and for that I will forever be grateful. Thanks for your love and care, Daddy.

I would also like to thank each and every person who donated to my GoFundMe campaign to help me raise money for the publishing of this book. Trust me, this would not have been possible without your contributions.

Special thanks to my cousin, Horace Halloway, for your financial and continued support.

Special thanks to Conclusio House Publishing—Kerri-Ann and her team—for bringing my very first book to life. I do not have the words in me to express the gratitude I feel. You are exceptional, and I appreciate you, and the work that you do, so much.

Finally, cheers to all my well-wishers, all of those who did not believe in me, and all who contributed as well as added to my triumphs or struggles, to all the doors that were closed on me, and to all the new ones that opened. To all who said I would not be successful without a Master's or PhD, watch me win! To all who contributed, in any shape or form, to the distribution of this book, I am, because you are. **Thank you. Thank you. Thank you!**

Table of Contents

Foreword	x
Chapter 1 ~ No Worries	1
Chapter 2 ~ Early Years of the Family Struggle	9
Chapter 3 ~ Noticing Father's Absence	15
Chapter 4 ~ Education Is the Key, But Why Was Sex on My Mind?	22
Chapter 5 ~ No Contact	28
Chapter 6 ~ Land of Opportunity	35
Chapter 7 ~ Family Issues and Physical Abuse	46
Chapter 8 ~ Love and Healing	56
Chapter 9 ~ Discovering My Passion	70
Chapter 10 ~ Mental Illness, Suicide, & Depression	77
Chapter 11 ~ When You Think It's Peace & Safety, There Can Be Sudden Destructions. But I Am a HUSTLA!	87
~ An Open Letter to Mommy and Daddy	101
~ Healin' Scares	106
~ What's Coming Next	107

Foreword

"When life gives you lemons, make lemonade!"—do you remember this piece of advice? I have received and shared this advice on countless occasions, as I imagine you have as well. The concept is that when the circumstances of your life don't make sense for you, rather than resigning yourself to suffering, you can do something about it. This is a good way to describe what most successful people do. But when I reflect on Tasheka's journey, I realize that what is most inspiring about her is that she took her "lemons" and made "melons," not lemonade. Don't panic, I will break that down for you.

You see, the idea of making lemonade has become so common that it is actually the norm. Everybody makes lemonade. What Tasheka did was so outside of the box that it could be considered miraculous. From her humble beginnings in a tough inner-city community in Kingston, Jamaica, to sitting on the Premier's Council of Youth Opportunities, providing advice to the most powerful politician in the most powerful province in Canada, Tasheka has taken this improbable journey and has managed to give hope and a sense of direction to young and old alike across the Greater Toronto Area along the way.

When I heard that she was writing a book, my first thoughts were Really? At such a young age? What could she possibly have to write about? Then I began to reflect on our conversations and the parts of her journey to adulthood that she so graciously shares with me.

I remember attending a youth leaders' meeting and observing a young woman engaging with her peers. Her presence was commanding far beyond her years, which I later learned was much younger than I had originally assumed. She was commanding without being loud. A colleague of mine brought her over to me and said, "Danavan, you must meet Tasheka. This sister is doing some amazing things in the City." Truer words were never spoken.

Tasheka's story of hardship and struggle became the blueprint for Healin' Scars, a mentorship program supporting youth healing through the arts to develop life skills, while addressing issues such as Mental Health. Tasheka's ability to hold fast to who she is has reinforced for me a belief that has governed my approach to youth engagement for over a decade—"Identity matters" and "Knowledge of self matters." As a young black woman coming of age in a society where mainstream and subcultures—hip-hop, dancehall, social media, Hollywood, and the internet—often create an unattainable image for black women and present a misogynistic model of masculinity, Tasheka managed to carve out a platform for herself to grow and become a dynamic leader.

When you read this story, you will be inspired to make "melons." You will understand that you can take the elements of your life and rearrange them into something that works for you. Just like taking the letters in L-E-M-O-N-S and creating M-E-L-O-N-S. After reading Tasheka's story, it will be that simple for you, too!

Walk Good.

Danavan Samuels
Manager, Healthy Kids Strategy
City of Toronto

No Worries   1

"Rudy! Bammy! Wake up! It's time for school!" screamed my mother. "Mi tired fi tell you to go to yuh bed when night comes. Wake up, and go inna the bathroom. It's six o'clock already!"

It was like this every morning as I awoke for school, followed by, "Hurry up, and come take at least two spoons of the tea or porridge. Mi can't afford fi you get gas, so you try come and take at least two spoons of something warm before you go." Then she concluded with, "Okay, you ready now. Go. And remember when you are crossing to make sure you wait for Crossy (the crossing-guard) to cross you. Don't just cross on your own."

"Alright, Mommy. Lata," I usually responded on my way out.

As I walked down my street, I would greet my neighbours. "Morning, Miss Silvie! Morning, Miss Peggy! Morning, Miss Phyllis! Morning, Miss Julie! Morning, Miss Lavern!"

Miss Silvie lived in the first house right next to mine, with a red gate and greyish-brown walls. She would either be hanging up clothes or just getting ready to go to work. Miss Silvie was bald, and she was of medium build, shorter and older than my mom. She was always going to work, but I never knew what her job was.

Miss Peggy lived in the third house, next to Miss Silvie. Miss Peggy was a sienna-skinned woman with two kids, both older than me. In our lane (we use the word lane to describe smaller streets that are not main roads) at the time, Miss Peggy's was one of the better-off families, with a nice house and a dog named Moses, which I hated because I was scared of dogs.

Miss Peggy's children's names were Mike and Chin-Chin. Mike had astute skills in drawing, so any art homework I had I would always bring to Mike. Although Mike had his own homework at times, he never hesitated to help me with mine. We used to sit on a wooden stool and use a piece of plywood with a gas cylinder to hold it up as a table for the drawing. At the time, Miss Peggy was a seller of gas cylinders, so we always used the empty ones.

Chin-Chin was Miss Peggy's first child, who was a few years older than me. She was short with smooth chocolate skin and natural hair. We ended up going to the same primary and junior high school, where I would always try to hang out with her and her friends, all of whom were obviously older than me. I was almost like a mini Chin-Chin at school; wherever she was, I was right behind her. She would always take me to see her boyfriend at the time, which was pretty cool because he was humble and popular throughout the community. Many people always talked about her for having a boyfriend older than her, but there was one thing about Chin-Chin—she did not care too much about what people had to say about her; she just lived her life for herself.

Next down the lane was Miss Phyllis, the lane's most disliked old woman. She was the grandmother of my best friend at the time, Shu-Shu, who was a year older than me. Shu-Shu and I were very close. We were often compared by the neighbours and our family members, but nevertheless, we were very close.

People disliked Miss Phyllis because she was a very rude and miserable woman, and most of the community gossiped that she practiced *obeah*, otherwise known as witchcraft. My siblings and I were not allowed to speak of the rumours about Miss Phyllis inside our home, simply because my mother did not believe in the practice of witchcraft. To her, those kinds of conversations were not for children anyway, especially for me, because Miss Phyllis used to take me, Shu-Shu, and Mokii (her youngest grandchild) to a place called Rockfort Mineral Bath in Kingston, Jamaica, once a year.

The Rockfort Mineral Bath is a known Jamaican facility that includes beautiful picnic areas, a large pool, and mineralized water flowing out of rocks, which lead into streams that have a variety of fish swimming around. In the city where I am from, it was not often that we would get to go to a pool. However, Miss Phyllis provided us with that opportunity once a year, so I had no choice but to respect her and be grateful.

Miss Julie housed what I would call the "short family," with two daughters and two sons. I doubt anyone in that family was over 5'5". They had the biggest house on the lane, because the father lived in America for a while and would send them money. They were able to build up their home up to three stories. How ironic it was that the shortest family had the biggest house. He also sent barrels full of food and necessities for the family. Although they were the most fortunate family in the area, Miss Julie was always humble and kind. Whenever she received the barrels, she never hesitated to send me a few things out of it. I don't think she did the same with everyone on the lane, because although she was humble, she was never very friendly with everyone and usually chose to keep to herself. I was also the only child on the lane allowed to go inside her house, which in itself was like a privilege. Because it was the biggest house in the area, everyone always wondered what the inside looked like.

Directly down the lane, beside Miss Julie, lived Miss Lavern, who was a single mother. Her son's name was Andre, a.k.a. Prezi. Prezi and I became very close when I was in grade six. My clearest memory of Prezi and myself was the first time I ever held a gun. I was so young and so scared that I almost had a nervous breakdown. I did not know where he got it from or any information about it. All I could think to myself was, *Oh, man! I am actually holding a gun!*

Those were just a few neighbours from my community. The list of "mornings" went on the same, day after day. It was usually a twenty minute walk to get to the main road, sometimes even longer if we had to stop and wait for schoolmates. Every weekday morning, I would walk at least a mile from my home to attend my school. At the age of three, I was attending the Mennonite Basic School (otherwise known as kindergarten). I can remember those days as if they were yesterday, because then I was at absolute peace in an uncomplicated life. My only responsibilities were as follows: walk to school; get good grades; stay on the sidewalk; make sure Crossy crossed me; keep my uniform clean; eat my breaks (snacks at snack time); and, last but not least, never walk without shoes.

To this day, I still laugh about one of my clearest memories of this time in my life. I was in class two at four years of age. And one day while we were all in class, it started raining cats and dogs, so hard that even the teachers wanted to get out of the school as soon as they could. I watched as some the children had their taxis or parents pick them up and speed off. The issue at the time was that I had to walk home along with a few other kids whose parents did not have cars and could not afford taxis to pick them up. Like all the other kids I was rolling with at the time, this was the time of our lives, because we loved when it rained and we could all walk home and play. When our teacher allowed us to leave, we all ran out in excitement, took our shoes off, put them in our bags, and walked in the rain barefoot for almost a mile in the dirty street water.

Remember how one of my responsibilities was never to walk without my shoes? Right. I knew my mother was not going to like that idea, but at the time, I didn't care. I just wanted to join the fun, and so I did. That is one of the greatest things about being a child—you have no worries, except that if you were disobedient, you would get your ass busted.

Life was just all fun and games then. Even though we didn't live in the most upscale conditions with granite countertops, hot water to shower, and a refrigerator filled with food like most homes, it was paradise, for me and my friends at least.

When I finally arrived home that day, I walked right into my mother. I was soaked with water, my nose was sniffling, and my eyes were fiery red. She was not happy!

"Weh yuh shoes, likkle girl?" she asked in a raised voice. "Yuh think mi can afford fi take you to any hospital if you get sick inna hawd times like this? Mi ago buss yuh ass, so take off yuh uniform and come right back to mi!"

That was the end of that. I got a good beating, and I never walked without shoes another day in my life!

Let me slow it down a little bit and introduce myself. I am the third child of four on both my parents' sides. My given name is Tasheka Mason. *Tasheka* means *"wisdom, prone to self-sacrifice, and a peacemaker."* *Mason* is from an old French word of German origin meaning *"to make"* or *"stone worker."* According to the Akan day names, my day name is Adjua, which is connected to the day I was born. A Monday. This means *"peacemaker, humorous, devoted to helping others, and responsible"*—all of which describe me perfectly. I couldn't have done a better job describing myself on my own.

I was born after three hours of labour in my father's house in a community called Tivoli Gardens, and I was rushed to the Kingston Public Hospital. There my queen, Fredericka Thompson, my mother, spent three days before being released. I have to admit, I don't know how my mother feels, but as I grew up I would notice those "threes" surrounding me. I was born after three hours of labour, on the third day of the new year, as the third child for both parents, and was held for three days in the hospital before release.

I immediately questioned my purpose in life. I was raised in a small community of people called Cassava Piece, which is located at 193½ Constant Spring Road in Kingston 8, St. Andrew, Jamaica.

I was the only child for my father on my mother's side and the only child for my mother on my father's side. My mother's first two children were with the same man, and my father's first two children were with the same woman. Then there was me. I was the black sheep of the family. It wasn't really because of all the threes surrounding my name, but because of my journey—the journey that started in Cassava Piece. Like many other small communities in Jamaica at that time, we were not rich, nor extremely poor, nor middle class. We were in the surviving class, if there is such a category.

When I was between the ages of six and eleven, I attended primary school from grade one to six, which was a bit farther from my basic school. By the time I was six years old, the walk did not bother me at all. It had now become a routine that I was conditioned to, and I didn't even notice anymore that I was walking that far, five days a week, just to get an education, sometimes even on a partially empty stomach.

Let me tell you a little bit about the dynamics of my immediate family at the time. There were only four of us—my mother, my brother, my sister, and me. Up until I was about eight years old, we lived in a tenement yard, which is a big yard that has multiple houses and is semi-detached with no gates or fences to ensure privacy. Each home had one bathroom for everyone, and each family had their own coal stove or two burner stoves to cook their individual meals. We lived in a small board house with two and a half "bedrooms." I say "bedrooms" because I don't even know if that is the right word to describe what they were, or if they were just partitions in a whole space with a roof.

Nonetheless, we were just another family trying to survive. Fredericka never allowed us to be short of love at any time at all, and she taught us to love one another, despite our living conditions. She used to preach that even when we were down and in distress that we should never let anyone know and should always wear a smile, because God would always come through for us. She knew that with the drive and ambition she had we would not be in that condition for long. Cleary we weren't.

What I loved most about living in a tenement yard was that even though it was one yard with about five to ten board houses, the majority of the families had children. So, as children, we were never bored, unless we got into trouble and were not able to go outside and play. Fredericka was a strong believer in the African proverb, "It takes a village to raise a child."

Growing up at a tender age in a place like Cassava Piece, everyone knew who you were and whom you belonged to. Regardless of the horror stories you might have heard about the ghettos in Jamaica, I grew up in Cassava Piece and was able to walk around anytime at night without having to worry about being raped, kidnapped, or shot. In our community, the children were like loose cannons running wild, and we were definitely raised by the community members a majority of the time. There was nothing you could do in the dark, and even if you tried, you would get caught one way or another. The news would quickly get to your parent(s) or whichever family you belonged to. A community member was able to send you home if they thought you were out too late or if you were doing something wrong. They could beat you as if *they* were your parent(s), and then send you home to get another dose from your own parent(s), without them even asking you what happened. At that time in our community, if an adult disciplined you, then you must've done something wrong—no ifs, ands, or buts. I, of course, would get my little dose of beatings here and there, even while I enjoyed the sweet days of being a child with no worries.

I remember one day my friend, Kren-Kren, and I were up the street from my house, and there was a little scrimmage soccer game going on. Jimmy made it his pleasure to always call me and send me home when I was having fun. It's like he liked being an older brother, just to do that and annoy me. So, anyway, I was just chilling, enjoying the game with my friend, when my big brother, Jamar, a.k.a. Jimmy, came and said, "Erica a call yuh! She seh come dung now!" (Translation: *Fredericka is calling you and she said you should come now.*) Now, I was obviously not ready to go home yet, because who wants to go home so early and then hear from your friends the next day what happened after the game.

So I said, "Mi hear yuh, and mi soon guh dung!" (Translation: *I hear you, and I will go down soon.*)

As usual, my brother was not having that, so he started roughing me up in front of his friends, just doing and saying stuff big brothers do when they think you may have forgotten that they are older than you. So, obviously, as the little sister named Rudy, I rebelled. One thing led to another, and before I knew it, I said "Bomborass!"—a Jamaican cuss word—in one of my sentences.

At that point, Jimmy was standing in front of me, but I felt a sudden slap on my arm followed by, "Likke girl, yuh think yuh a big woman? Yuh fi hear when yuh bigga bredda talk to yuh!" (Translation: *Little girl, do you think you are a big woman? You should listen when your older brother talks to you!*) This was coming from one of the community members, Paulette, who was a longtime friend of my mother. This was how it usually went with me, and then I would head right into another ass whooping from my mother.

I must say, however, that it was those types of disciplinary actions that made most of us have manners and respect towards people, especially our elders. This sort of incident occurred on many occasions. I can even remember coming home from church on a Sunday afternoon and, having stopped to play with my friends, Jimmy came again, just because he knew that when I was not home he was the one who had to run errands for our mother.

He came and said, "Look how long church ova! Weh yuh nuh guh dung and guh change yuh clothes?" (Translation: *Church has been done a long time now. Why don't you go home and change your clothes?*)

I said, "No, low mi nuh. Yuh nuh see mi a do summn? And Mommy know seh mi up yah." (Translation: *Leave me alone. Can't you see that I am doing something? And Mommy knows I am here.*)

He did not like when he couldn't have his own way, because he thought our mom gave me too much leeway, something he and my big sister, Tammy a.k.a. Mummy, did not get too much of. So, he went home and told my mother that I was sitting with my friends and watching while they ate their Sunday dinner, as if I didn't have any of my own. I know you can guess what happened next. Of course, he came back for me, and when I got home, I got a scolding without questioning. Mother had so much pride that she didn't even want to hear my side of the story. She just wanted to make sure I was not making it seem as if she couldn't feed me.

I never hung around my friends' houses while they ate, again. Every time their dinnertime came around and I was there, I made sure to make my way home.

Lesson:

~ *Manners and respect will take you a long way.*

~ *The truth is some of us won't know the value of our parents' disciplinary actions until we're older, when it is sometimes a little too late.*

Early Years of the Family Struggle   2

Along with being a strict parent, my mother, Fredericka, was a very hard worker, who worked in a variety of different places throughout her life, from banks to bars. At this particular time, she was working at two places—a Free Zone (a factory with Chinese owners, where they sew clothing in a sweatshop for about ten to twelve hours, working for next to nothing), and as a domestic worker, cleaning rich people's houses. Therefore, she was not home a lot, which led to my brother and me having to be raised by the second runner-up, my eldest sister, Tammy.

She called all the shots when Mommy wasn't home. She would wash my hair, comb it, iron my clothes—if Mommy didn't get a chance to do so overnight—and, of course, whoop my ass whenever I got in trouble, which I did quite often. For that reason, my grandmother gave me the nickname "Rudy," which has stuck with me to this day. Tammy was my super-woman, after Mommy, of course. Due to the socio-economic ghetto lifestyle that was our reality, Tammy, unlike me, was not able to attend school, because she was too busy being a parent and a role model to her younger siblings. Sometimes there was not enough income in our family to support three children attaining an education. Therefore, she had no choice but to lose the majority of her schooling due to our harsh reality. She also missed out on her social life due to my mother's strict parentage.

I can vividly remember when my mother stopped working at the factory while in the process of building our new *wall house* (a house made of cement blocks) all by herself, which was a very big deal, especially for me as a child. It meant that now I would have a gate and my own bathroom. I must admit that I was a bit jealous of some of my friends, whose parents already had their wall houses, but now I would be a part of the concrete house movement that was going on.

The factories were closing down at this point, so they sent everyone home without any notice or pay. My mother came home, called me from outside where I was playing, and gathered my other two siblings as well. Fredericka was a very secretive woman, and again she taught us that no matter how hungry we were or how many problems we had, we should keep it inside our family. We were all we had. There were no uncles or aunts to run to on a regular basis, so we kept our issues as one.

When she told us the bad news, I didn't really understand it quite like my brother and sister, all I wanted to know was what was going to happen to our wall house. She said the only temporary solution that she could think of was to ask the man that she did domestic work for if he could give her more time or raise her pay. We all told her to ask him, and so she did. He agreed, because he liked the way she worked, and she explained to him that she wanted to finish our house. He offered her more time as a live-in worker until she finished making the house. This was good for her, but it was not so good for us. As a live-in worker, she only had maybe one or two days off, if she was lucky. This also meant more work for Tammy, and absolutely no schooling.

However, we all appreciated her boss for giving her the extra work. I will never forget that man. His name was Mr. Abrahams. He was a politician, a member of the Jamaican Labour Party (JLP). I went to work with her one Saturday. The walk to his house up in Norbrook (an upscale community) was very long, but once you were there, it wasn't such a long walk. The house was about two-and-a-half stories, painted in green and white, with a swimming pool and a huge backyard. It was one of the best houses I had ever stepped foot in. Enter the gates…royalty! He had workers for everything. Apparently, he even had painters come in three times per year to repaint the whole property. We were happy Mommy was one of his employees.

So, our new house was finally finished. It was two minutes away from where we used to live, on a piece of "captured land." Before you knew it, we were just like all the others, living in a concrete house with our own gate and stuff. However, there was still a problem. Now that the house was finished and my mother's boss kept his promise to help her out until its completion, she was now getting fewer hours at work and barely making enough money to make ends meet for all of us.

Whenever my father visited me, which was rare, he would leave a little money, but it was still a struggle. Even though we had a nice little house, we still could not afford gas for the stove, so the majority of the time we would cook our dinner on a coal stove outside. The most embarrassing part about this was when I had to go purchase the coal, and everyone would see me walking home with it. I would usually walk with at least four black plastic bags to put it in, but that still didn't hide it enough.

Times were so hard that sometimes we would go to bed having eaten rice and butter for dinner. For breakfast, on good days, we had condensed milk mixed in water and some corn flakes. On regular days, it would just be sugar and tea with some tough crackers, if we had any, or bread and butter. I was not even able to get a decent amount of lunch money; sometimes none at all. I was the child that still went to school, with or without, because I knew I had to get an education. Even if I did not know a lot of what was going on in our home, I knew we needed more money, and according to my mother, a good education would lead to some decent money. She would never forget to stress that I was probably going to be the only one out of her three children who would have a proper education. That weight of expectation was on my shoulders for a while, so I had no choice but to go to school, with or without lunch money.

I, however, had some pretty cool friends who would share with me when I would lie and say I left my lunch money at home or tell some other white lie as to why I had no lunch that day. These were the days when a friend would cut out half of their lunch box and give their friends some of their food. It was embarrassing when you had the smaller half of the box, because everyone knew that meant you were the one without money.

As I look back now, I realize no one really cared much, because they knew how hard the country was. Sometimes my happiest days in school were when I knew I was going home to a meal and I would have lunch money for the next day. My favourite meals at the time were corned beef and white rice, liver or kidney and white rice, curry chicken back and dumplings, and on the rare times when we would have them, fish or oxtail on a Sunday, which I couldn't even get much of because it had to stretch for the whole family.

Mommy never hid money from us; we knew when we had and when we did not. Therefore, we acted accordingly. I could not tell my friends that we sometimes had nothing to eat at home; my mother would have killed me. She enforced pride in us as if it was law, and we had to live by it, day by day, and not break it. Even in our household, as siblings we had simple disagreements here and there, but we could not ever fight, as my mother taught us to live as one unit and love one another. If one was hungry, all of us were. If one could not spell, all of us had to try to teach that one how to, and that one would usually be me, because I was the baby. Jimmy had to stay up with me late nights until I learned to spell properly.

If one had a shoe, the other should be able to wear it—meaning Tammy and me. That would piss her off so much, because she hated when I wore her clothes, especially without her permission. I found that weird and funny at the same time, because she was the one to say she could not have me going on the road "looking just any way." I had to look decent. So if I was going somewhere and she had something nice, Mommy or I would sneak it out and then she would get mad at me, even though she had admonished me only a few days earlier that I should always make sure I looked decent when going anywhere. Experiencing life in those conditions made me appreciate every millisecond of the life I have now.

The struggle was real. Only someone who experiences it knows it. There were times when I would wake up and see my mother crying tears because she had no idea where our next meal would come from. The only person who could have assured her that we would be okay was Tammy. Even though they argued every now and then, which would make me cry or have a nervous breakdown because I hated to see it, they never hesitated to be there for each other as a support system during our roughest times.

Speaking of rough times, I can remember vividly when I was about seven or eight years old, and Tammy was missing from the house for about a day and a half. My mother said she had sent her to see one of our family members to take a break from our community and to ask for some money. She said she had gone to a place called Papine Tavern, which was a little bit beyond the Bob Marley Museum on Hope Road.

I noticed my sister's absence immediately because my mother was very strict, and if one of us was gone somewhere for that long, there had to be a really good reason. We weren't allowed to even sleep at our neighbour's house when we lived in the big yard, and the houses were attached.

Anyway, my sister was away, and my mother was just a bit

uneasy, because we didn't have phones back then to call and see how things were going. So this was like my sister's first time of freedom, except when she got to go to school about two to three times a week, if that. Tammy finally returned the next day, and she was a day later than when Mommy had expected her so, of course, she started to get grilled about where she had been and what had happened.

Let me tell you, Fredericka was a no-joke mother, man. If you were living under her roof and you were a female, anywhere you went, she would literally open up your legs and check to see what was going on between your legs when you returned home. I don't know what she was looking for, but she looked anyway. At this point my sister was around seventeen, and my mother told her to go take off her clothes and come open her legs on the bed, but she refused. I had never seen my sister refuse anything that my mother told her to do, so I was surprised at her refusal to do as she was told.

My mother then started to put her on the bed and open her legs by force. I can remember, as clear as day, the image that was painted in front of me at such a tender age. After all the struggle of trying to get Tammy's legs open, all I could see was blood flowing from my sister like a stream. She had blood all over her undershorts and her panties. It even got on her skirt. By the time I was able to process what I had just seen, my mother had a water hose beating the hell out of my sister, cussing, and crying at the same time.

I had never seen my mother cuss and cry at the same time, so I knew it was serious. From my understanding, and based on what Tammy had explained to me, she had lost her virginity that day with her boyfriend who lived close to one of our uncle's houses, and she did her dirt the first and only chance she got after being locked in for so many years.

Later on that month, Tammy was really sick and throwing up everything she ate. Yes, you guessed it. She was, unfortunately, pregnant after her first time. Mommy cried, cussed, and beat her again when she found out about the pregnancy. She even almost killed Tammy and my nephew. She was so upset that she used one of those blocks they used to build the house and threw it at her. Luckily, she dodged it, and it barely hit her, causing only minor scars to her body. Mommy then told her to keep the child because she didn't believe in abortions, and even if she did, we couldn't afford it.

The family welcomed a beautiful, healthy baby boy on January

31ˢᵗ. Upon my sister's arrival at the house, I laid eyes on the most pure and divine human being I have ever met. He laughed when he saw me. He curled up in my arms, fearless and tearless, coolly and calmly.

We clicked immediately. To this day, Rushane Stewart, my first nephew, is probably my most favourite person on the face of the earth, and Tammy's main reason for never giving up in life.

Lesson:

~ The difficulties of yesterday are the motivation of today.

A Note to Parents:

No matter what your financial situation is in life, pay close attention to your children. Ask them questions. Know about their social life, what their interests are, and so forth. This is very important to their development, to know that you trust them. Stop talking down to your children and start talking with your children.

A Note to Mothers:

Try your best to have a father figure/male role model present. Even if it means constantly surrounding your children with positive male figures. No matter how strong and how powerful you are, a mother cannot be a father. No doubt you can be a phenomenal single mother, but you can never be a father. There will always be that part missing, which will have your child questioning what that experience of love would feel like from the missing figure. Therefore, you as the single parent have to be able to have open and honest conversations with them.

Noticing Father's Absence 3

During summer, Christmas, and all other holidays, I would get so excited because I got to spend time with my father's side of the family. My other siblings, as I mentioned previously, were Tee, my father's first child, who was four years older than my brother, Damion, who was the same age as me. In rural Jamaica, in a place called Silent Hill in Manchester, a few hours away from Kingston, I would usually spend time with them if I was not at my father's house in Kingston, where we basically visited different stepmothers daily.

My favourite part, other than spending time alone with my dad on the journey, was stopping at Melrose Hill to get roasted yam with melted butter and saltfish. There were multiple vendors on the same strip, all selling the same thing. As the journey continued, we would pass street fruit vendors with the yellowest bananas, the fattest oranges, and the juiciest watermelons. I would always marvel looking from my window at the vendors, wondering from where and how far they travelled each day to sell their goods. Upon arriving in Silent Hill, where my grandmother lived, it was a very different scenery from Kingston. Kingston was industrial, with business buildings and main roads, and it just felt like a city. Compared to Kingston, this place looked poor. However, to me, it was luxury.

My grandmother's house was a nice two-story concrete house with a street-side shop. And across the valley, you could see a whole different parish called St. Ann, with beautiful houses and lush greenery. Grandma's house had a verandah, a kitchen, and four big rooms that housed my brother, Damion, and my cousin, Darren, in one, Tee and Cousin Kimesha in another, my grandma in another, and my grandpa in another. My grandparents were married with seven children, for God knows how long, and twenty-nine grandchildren, and a couple of great-grandchildren. Could you believe they slept in separate rooms? Nevertheless, my grandmother respected, washed, cooked, and cleaned for her husband. Although he was an alcoholic and she was a faithful Christian woman, she made sure her husband was never lacking in anything.

Another beautiful thing about being in the country was that food was never an issue, not for me at least. I could go to an aunt or uncle's house, whenever my grandmother was not finished cooking, to get something to eat. I ate day in and day out because this lifestyle was not available in Kingston, although my mother did her best to provide for us.

The big family environment was always cool to me. It was nice to be able to see many children, who were somewhat related to me, in one place, playing and having fun without a thought about where our next meal would come from. Life there was just about playing, showering, eating, and sleeping, and like in Kingston, going to church on Sundays was mandatory.

Even though I loved the country so much, I can never forget the first time I was told I was going to stay there without my dad. I cried for three days straight, and I was taken from one family member's house to the next, until they finally calmed me down. I was still eager to go back every holiday. Even though I used to hate having to leave my family, I still loved spending time alone with my dad on the way back.

Unbelievably, my mother and other people always said I was the spitting image of my father. I acted just like him and always took his side, no matter what the situation was. During the ride home, I usually got time to connect with him on a more personal level, talk to him about what was going on at school, and let him know if my mom beat me, and anything else that I was interested in at the moment. We talked like two friends, even though I was so young. He treated me like his precious little gem, showing me all the attention and love in the world during rides to and from the country. Sadly, this was the only time I could remember us connecting on an understanding level and, of course, I cherished those memories along with the view of beautiful Jamaica on the way.

I can never forget this one time I arrived in the country. I would usually drop my stuff inside my room and give my grandmother a big kiss and storm out to go play with the other kids. But this time

I did all of that, and after playing for a couple hours, I went inside to ask my grandmother, "Weh daddy deh?" (Translation: Where is my father?)

Her reply was, "You know your father is not staying here. He is long gone. Go freshen up, so I can give you your dinner and go lay down."

This did not sit well with me, because I was getting older and more curious. I was confused and didn't understand why he would always want to leave so quickly when I barely got to see him in general, probably like once every other month, if I was lucky. Looking back at it now, I guess I was lucky because some kids never got to see their fathers at all. I wasn't going to sweat it; I was a child. I knew he was going to come get me in a couple of weeks, but while I was there, all I could think about was that it had come to my attention that my father was kind of pawning me off every time I went to spend time with him.

Memories of previous holidays resurfaced in my mind, like times when I was supposed to go to his house for at least a month with Tee and Damion. We slept at his house with his girlfriend, but he wouldn't sleep there. We would see him a day or two later, and even if he brought us out on the road with him, which he would do once in a while, he would just bring us to another girlfriend's house to stay for a little while then go. Believe me, he had a couple of them. At the time, it didn't really bother us because these women would usually have children, and we would rather be playing with them than staying in my father's boring house. Plus, these women would spend money on us like there was no tomorrow. We really enjoyed that; therefore, we didn't really care about his absence.

After thinking back to the day I asked my grandmother for him, I can recall that that night Tee had slept at an aunt's house, and I was at Grandma's house in the room alone. I had some time alone to think, and when my father's absence came to mind, I started to cry. At the time, I couldn't explain why I was crying, but now I know I just felt abandoned by my father all of a sudden. I wasn't sweating it though. Mommy had taught me to keep things to myself, so I did just that. I kept it to myself and played it cool until weeks later when my father came to pick me up and drop me home.

Looking back, every time I returned to my regular life of survival in Cassava Piece, I realized two things: firstly, my family in the country would always complain and say my father spent more time with me than Tee and Damion, and that I was his favourite, which

I could never understand, because like I said, the longest time we would spend together was on the ride to and from the country. Secondly, I started hanging out and playing mostly with the male kids in my community and doing what they were doing. I guess you can label this as the beginning of my "tomboy phase."

Mommy didn't really bother me about it. I guess she was still traumatized by Tammy's pregnancy. Her only rule was that if I was playing with all the male kids, we had to play at my house where she could see us, which was not a problem for us at all. We just wanted to do what kids did at the time. But this also had Tammy and Jamar thinking that I was my mother's favourite and that she spoiled me

Speaking of which, I had one neighbour who was my only female friend, and she is going to be very surprised when she reads this, but that's cool. She is still one of my very good friends to this day— Miss. Phyllis's granddaughter, Shu-Shu. I was always very jealous of this girl. Growing up, she lived with both parents in a nice house and would travel back and forth from America to Jamaica. It was a very big deal when someone travelled to America and came back with all the cool stuff that looked very expensive. Shu-Shu had a perfect life in my eyes, and I would always dream of having a life like that, because nothing was more important to a child than seeing both parents together doing groceries, going to bed, waking up together, and so forth.

I remember when there were rumours going around in our community that her father was cheating on her mother, but my mother taught us to mind our own business, and so we did. Therefore, Shu-Shu's family business was not spoken of in our household.

One day, my family and I were all inside sleeping when we heard a loud BOOM! We ran outside. It was the police knocking out the window of one of our neighbours' houses, where they had received a call that someone was in the house dying, and by the time they got in, the person was already dead. Shu-Shu's family seemed to be taking this the hardest, and so I asked Tammy what was going on. She said, "Cappa dead ova Julee dem house." Shu-Shu's father had apparently died in the person's house that he was allegedly cheating on her mother with. I had never seen Shu-Shu so devastated. She cried that night, and no one in our immediate surroundings slept. We mourned with the family all night long.

All I could have done at the time was sit beside her and hold her hand. I had nothing to say. I felt so bad for her. Yet, at the time, all I could think about was if I would've cried and mourned the same way she did if my father had passed. I mean, we barely saw or did anything with each other. We didn't do the groceries. We didn't travel, except to the country every few months. He definitely did not wake up in the same house as me. Though, on the other hand, I cried for him every time I would get my ass whooped by Mommy. As bad as I felt for her, I was more worried about how she and her little sister were going to adapt to the one-parent household.

I thought to myself, *Man, this is what I was jealous over! Do I still want her life?* The days following his death were really sad for the whole lane, and I will never forget those moments we all came together in support of her family.

Another day that really stood out to me was when I was in about the third or fourth grade. At the time, my teacher, Ms. Alexander, who looked like a typical librarian with her glasses, her hair tied in a taut bun, and dark skin, called me out of the classroom and said my father was outside. I would be able to go after I finished taking the notes off the chalkboard. Now, in Jamaica, when you had a parent that drives a car and shows up at your school early to pick you up, he or she would bring you a popsicle or something so that you would be all excited to show off to your friends. Believe me when I say I was more than excited! As I said, I didn't see my father often, and whenever I did, I would be glad to.

I finished my notes extremely fast that time and stormed out of the classroom. I ran into my father's arms while he sat with the driver's door open, and he welcomed me into his arms. I noticed, though, that there was no popsicle or sweet treats in his hand. He only had a brown envelope.

I said to him, "Daddy, yuh come pick me up? Weh wi ago?" *(Translation: Daddy, did you come to pick me up? Where are we going?)*

"No," he said. "Mi come drop off dis to yuh before mi leave." *(Translation: I came to drop this off to you before I leave.)* He dangled the envelope in his hands. "Gi it to yuh teacher and take it from her after school and put it inna the small zip part of yuh bag. Gi it to yuh madda, and mek sure yuh nuh lose it." *(Translation: Give it to your teacher and take it from her after school and put it into the small zipped part of your bag. Give it to your mother, and make sure you don't lose it.)* He kissed me on the forehead, hugged me, and then he drove off.

This is my most fragile memory of my father, and I hold that to this day. When I watched him leave, my mind was filled with confusion and worry. I asked myself why he couldn't give it to her himself. Why did he come all the way to my school? After school, I went straight home just like every other day. The only difference was that this time I was eager to see my mother to find out what was going on. I gave my mother the envelope as instructed, and she immediately said, "Mi neva know him did a go weh so quick." *(Translation: I did not know he was leaving so soon.)*

Still confused, I asked her, "Mommy, a weh Daddy a go? Him nah come back?" *(Translation: Mommy, where is Daddy going? Is he going to come back?)*

"Him a go foreign." *(Translation: He is going to a foreign country.)* "Him might come back, but not for now," she replied humbly and subtly.

"So why im gimme di envelope, and what inna it?" I asked. *(Translation: So why did he give me the envelope, and what is in it?)*

"It's money," she said as she opened it. "Him did just come a yuh school fi tell yuh seh him gone, an leave this money for you—a ten thousand dollar inna it," she said again, so humbly. *(Translation: He just came to tell you that he was leaving and to leave this money for you—it's ten thousand dollars.)*

I left that conversation at that, and I just knew at the time that I couldn't cry because that was not the emotion I was feeling. I knew crying couldn't make him stay. I knew I had to deal with it and move on just like everything else that happens in a life of trying to survive when obstacles come your way. You deal with them like a soldier and just move on, so I did without any further questions, concerns, or emotions. I didn't see him often anyway, so I just knew I had to deal with his absence for now and just move on.

Lesson:

~ *Family is supposed to be a harmonized unit. Whenever one is not singing, no one knows; because the harmony is so powerful, you can't even notice that someone is missing.*

~*Communicate with and enjoy the times that you have with close family and friends, because you can lose someone in the blink of an eye. Just like Shu-Shu lost her father, and mine left without warning or expectation.*

4
Education Is the Key, But Why Was Sex on My Mind?

"Rudy pass! Rudy passed for Camperdown High!" was all I can remember my sister screaming throughout the community, from top to bottom, on the phone telling my mother, and not hesitating to let the whole community know how proud she was of me. Of course, my mother left work and called my father and yelled the same thing.

The pressure of being in grade six and writing an exam that my future depended on, according to Jamaicans, was finally gone. This exam that was called Common Entrance in my sister's days and before, and is now called the GSAT (Grade Six Achievement Test) is a test done by all sixth graders in the county to challenge what they have learned throughout primary school. And depending on how well you do, you will be placed in the highest to the lowest ranking high schools in the country. Every family takes pride in every child around that time of the year. You become like a star child because they do any and everything to make sure you pass for the best high school.

After all the times of going to bed with next to nothing to eat, going to see men at nighttime who were friends of my mom to beg for lunch money for school the next morning, and attending as much extra lessons as I could, I was glad I wouldn't be walking long walks to school anymore. I would be taking the bus, and I was relieved all that walking would soon be over.

While my family celebrated my achievement, I wasn't quite interested in the celebration as much as they were. My mind was farther than where anyone could imagine a sixth grader who had just passed for a good school's mind ought to be. My mind was on *sex*. Yes, I said it, *sex*. But first, let me explain. There was a boy who was about three years older than me; his name was Tashane.

'Tashane vs. Tasheka,' I loved the sound of it. I wrote it all over my notebooks and wherever else I wrote. In my world at the time, I was in love.

You see, Tashane worked for the supermarket—a walking distance away from my house—during the summertime. If I tell you that those supermarket cameras didn't know my face, along with the supervisors, security guards, and cashiers, I would be lying.

Now, in my mind, I was starting high school after the summer, and I was grown. So, with my father not in the country and my mother working as much as she could, I had time to spend with my 'boyfriend.' Of course, by spending time, I meant with every dollar I got, I would go to the supermarket, just to say hi.

If my mom told me to just go to the shop, which is the third house from where we lived, I wouldn't go there. I would go all the way up to the supermarket, and I would also go up there after he was finished with work. We would talk and hug or cuddle before his bus came. Every chance I got, I was at that damn supermarket.

Now, let me tell you about the "relationship" Tashane and I had. It all started one day when I went to the supermarket, and when your parents sent you to the supermarket so often, after a while you kind of had an idea of what the boys who packed your bags looked like. One day, Davia, who was a friend of mine, and I went to the supermarket, and I noticed this dark, medium-built, bow-legged boy, whom we had never seen before. If you know me, you know I am a sucker for legs. I mean, they have to have some form of shape when a male stands. Anyway, unlike Davia, I was determined to find out who this young man was. Luckily for me, Davia lived right behind the supermarket, so whenever I wanted to go see Tashane, I would just ask to spend the day at Davia's house. Believe me, I took advantage of that. Around lunch time that day, I was at Davia's, and you know where I went. I saw him outside standing. My heart started pounding. We had said "hi" and "bye" a couple times before and while he packed my bags, but nothing serious. This time, however, was very serious. I had never seen him outside alone before. As I was walking towards him, I was a nervous wreck. When I finally got closer, he said, "What's up, stranger?"

As nervously as you can imagine, I said, "Nothing!"…and continued walking.

He held my hand and pulled me back and said, "Hold on likkle bit nuh!" (*Translation: Wait a sec!*)

I said, "Hold on fi wah? Mi busy." (Translation: What for? I'm busy.)

Of course, I played hard to get for a little while, but gave in eventually. At this point, I had no experience in how to deal with a boyfriend. All I knew was my sister had one and a few of my friends had as well. So I wanted a boyfriend, and I sure did get myself one. After that first encounter, we exchanged numbers, and we were now a "couple." Yeah, that's exactly how it went back then. Once you started talking to someone on the phone every day, you were a couple. No going out necessary. In my case, this was just constant visits to his place of work or play, regardless of being invited or not.

Tashane had asked me one day while we were under the tree at the supermarket, after he finished working, if I would have sex with him after I did my GSAT. He said if we did, he would never leave me or cheat on me. I told him I would think about it. That is why I had sex on my mind after that exam.

Now, mind you, the only time I had thought of, or rather witnessed, sex before that was one night when I was looking for Tammy and I peeked through her window. I saw her doing the nasty with my nephew's father. That image never left my mind. To this day I still laugh about it.

My mother, sister, and brother did not know about Tashane. However, my nephew did, because he was also a good excuse to go to the supermarket. Any money I had, I would say I was going to buy him ice-cream or something, and he knew the plan right then and there, even though he was only three years old or so. He knew that when we got there, Tashane would bring him the ice-cream, so he would sit by himself and eat while Tashane and I would stand under the tree, laughing and talking. He had no worries; he was just glad for the treat.

Tashane had a twin sister named Tashuana who knew about what we had going on. Whenever we had problems, she would deal with it. At that age, relationship problems were like, *why is he looking at or talking to other females?* Period. Tashuana, along with her older brother and younger sister, knew about me, so I was claiming wifey status at the time, because even his mother had a little idea. After visiting his house only one time, I had lied to my mother. I had come home late and, you guessed it, earned myself a buss ass. So trust me, this relationship thing was serious business. No joke, I was in love, or so I thought.

After not seeing Tashane for a few days after my GSAT results came out, he called and said, "So yuh nah gimmie the ting before you start high school?" (*Translation: Aren't you going to let us have sex before you start high school?*) For some reason, I did not answer, and the phone got cut off. I went straight into my bathroom and started to cry, telling myself that he was going to leave me, that I didn't know what I was going to do without him, that my life was nothing without him, and that he would hate me forever. I thought about every kiss on the cheek, hug, and squeeze we shared. I cried every chance I got alone and couldn't eat for days.

He finally answered my calls after a few days. By then, I didn't know what to say to him. I didn't even know if I still wanted to be his little girlfriend, so I continued talking to him while he was under the impression that we were going to do 'it.' This was just a coping mechanism for me. I couldn't completely cut him out of my life; I needed a slow transition. Then I remembered what happened to my sister and how devastated my mother was, so one day I called him and told him that I was not ready for sex yet, because I was not of age, and if he never wanted to talk to me again that was his business. I could hear how shocked he was that I told him that, so much so that he didn't even bother saying anything, he just hissed his teeth and hung up the phone. Before I knew it, a couple of my friends who were already in high school had already lost their virginities, so I was the oddball. I lied and told them that by grade nine I would try it.

Later that year, I started Camperdown High, and I loved that I was no longer walking to school. I would walk from my house through the back, which led me right back to the tenement yard, meet up with my good friend, Kren-Kren, whose school was close to mine. Then we would go through a little passage that led out to a place they called 'Back Piece' or 'Moses Corner.' Once we passed there, we would end up on a main road near a police station. From there, it was about a block from the station to the bus stop on Constant Spring Road. This was one of the few bus stops in Kingston that actually had a bus shed. In the mornings, the bus stop was usually packed with people from all different schools as well as people going to work.

There were two types of buses. One is government owned called JUTC (Jamaica Urban Transit Company). These are very similar to the busses in North America today. The others were smaller buses we liked to call Coasters or mini-buses. It was important to know that if you were going to work and you hated loud music and a bunch of school children being loud, your best choice would be to take the JUTC. School goers back in those times loved the Coasters; although they cost a little bit more money, they were generally just more fun.

However, for us, I remember having to wait for specific ones because some of them were actually lame with no up-to-date music. We used to always wait for either 'Sweet Champagne,' 'Metro,' or another one I cannot quite remember the name of, because these were what we called the 'hot' buses. I would take a bus from there to downtown and then a bus from downtown straight to my school, which was located on South Camp Road.

After a few weeks of class, I actually liked the school and my classmates. I was on the junior soccer team. Since I looked older than my age, I had friends that were older than me who would look out for me, one of which was the son of the famous dancehall artist Spragga Benz. I also had some pretty cool teachers, one of which was a well-known actor from the famous Jamaican movie *Dancehall Queen*. I had a few mandatory classes that I had no idea existed in Jamaica, like chess, French, and economics.

In the mornings, the whole school gathered outside in what we called Devotion, where the principal would address us, teachers checked to make sure we were wearing all the right attire—brown shoes, brown socks, and uniform three inches below the knee—and at the end of each term, our teachers presented us with "A" badges, which meant we'd received a significant number of A's that term.

I remember how during class my teacher would call us out in ranking order of who got the best to the worst grades. It was during these times that I realized there were actually people in my class who were a lot smarter than I was. There was this one girl, Janelle Walker, whom I will never forget. She was always first in the whole class. I knew my best friend, Jhevantee, had a thing for her, but everyone in class hated her around these times, whether they wanted to admit it or not. You know what else I hated? Math! I hated math! Something she loved. This gave a number of my classmates a better advantage over me. I think I was placed in the top three once or twice. Other than that, I was usually fifth, sixth, or even eighth out of about twenty-seven students.

> **Lesson:**
> *~ Not because your friends have done it, doesn't mean you should do it, too. Stay in your lane and go at your own pace; you would be surprised at what you discover along your journey.*

A Note to Parents:

Please be mindful of your children's whereabouts and the company they keep at all times, especially your young girls, regardless of age. Be open about the topic of sex; thoroughly explain the cons and why they should not even be thinking about it. Try your best not to keep them in the dark about things like sex, as they will find out elsewhere, and it is better you tell them than someone else.

5 No Contact

It had been years since my father left and, naturally, my mother started seeing someone else, whom, to be honest, I wasn't a fan of at all. I mean, you know how it goes—kids do not appreciate anyone with their mother but their father, especially girls. For me, it was a joyful and warm feeling whenever both my parents were in the same place laughing, talking, and looking happy, even if they weren't, and that was a feeling I wished to feel every day.

Let's just face it, that was all a dream. However, that person who tried to take my father's place was more like a nightmare. I never had a part in choosing him. My mother didn't even allow me to have an opinion on her choice, which I think I should have had the privilege of having, because he was going to be a part of my life, too. I resented my mother's choice for years.

It all started when the verbal fighting suddenly became a part of our everyday lives. He argued with my mother back to back, as if they were both females living in one house, menstruating at the same time. One thing I could say about my father then was that whenever my mother was mad at him and it seemed like it was going to be an argument, he would jump into his car and go for a spin and come back when he knew she was calm. But this sorry excuse of a man, not so much. The fighting continued on and off each time he visited, and I always wondered why my mother was still with this sissy. She was an independent woman and could do way better without him. Months had passed, and it was obvious that he was going nowhere but back and forth from his house to ours. I, along with my sister and brother, didn't like it, but we had to deal with it.

One day, I overheard Tammy and Mommy talking about a

baby. I didn't usually eavesdrop in their conversations, because I knew Mommy usually told us everything anyway. However, this particular conversation seemed sort of strange and somewhat top secret, so I was eager to know. Besides, my mother had been acting strangely leading up to my overhearing this conversation. I finally found the courage to ask them what was going on, and they both said she was over seven months pregnant. I was startled. I ran and began to cry; I felt defeated. Not only did I hate the father of the child at the time, but I was the baby in the family. You know how it goes when you've been the last child for so long; it is difficult to welcome another child who is now going to be considered the baby—not to mention how upset I was that she kept it from me for so long. It was actually unbelievable. My mother was a very slender woman, and her tummy was very small during her pregnancy.

After being very upset about the new addition to the family for weeks, not only calling my father to rant, but ignoring my mother as much as I possibly could, the baby was finally here, and to tell the honest truth, I stayed away from the child. I never touched her, lifted her, or fed her. I wanted nothing to do with the child. You can call this a selfish act and, as I look back, I would agree with you. However, at the time, I knew I was acting from a place of pain and resentment.

I came home from school one day, and the baby was lying in her crib while my mother was in the shower. She was crying so hard and her face was so red that you would think she had a permanent blush. As sad as it is for me to say today, I must tell you that I walked right past her, as if I didn't see her. It is funny how at the time I was so angry, and something serious could have been wrong with her but, because of my selfishness, I ignored her as if we didn't come from the same womb. I saw how it hurt my mother, but I didn't care. Now that I look back at it, I realize that Mommy didn't even cuss at me. I guess she knew how I felt and why I felt the way I did.

I would like to take the time out to say that this is not acceptable at all in any circumstance, and for that I want to apologize to my little sister, Symeka Wynter. Although she was too young to understand what was going on, I did, and regardless of her age, it was not fair to her that I hated my mother's decision to have her.

This shows how deeply our parents' life choices impact us as children, whether consciously or unconsciously. Well I am proud to say that right now as you read this, Symeka, or "Sym Sym" as we would like to call her, is the exact same person as the little girl that was called Rudy by her then peers. Can you believe it? When people call me from Jamaica they always remind me of how much alike we are and that they call her 'Little Rudy.' Not only does she remind the people in the community of me, but when I speak to her, she reminds me of me. Things my mother used to do to me, the ways she used to talk to me, and the problems she used to have with me are the exact same with her. Not only is she as rude as I was then, but she is also as smart as I was. According to her teachers, she is one of the smartest in her class. I am proud to say that she will soon be living with me, and I can't wait to groom her and help her as much as I can to not make the same mistakes I did.

Although I believe that it is important for everyone to make some mistakes to prove that they are not just living but they are also trying, the very first and most important step is that you try. Whether wrong or right, you can't say you didn't learn anything from trying.

Speaking of school, at Camperdown I knew a guy who had an aunt in my area that he used to live with. He remembered me from Cassava Piece as Fredericka's daughter, Rudy. The minute he saw me at school, we started hanging out more and even taking the bus to Half-Way Tree together.

When one day he finally admitted that he liked me, I was shocked. This guy was one of the guys the younger girls in Camperdown crushed over. He was tall, light-skinned with wavy hair, medium build, and had a bright Colgate smile to match his intelligence. I started getting butterflies. When I saw him in school, I ran. I just couldn't face him anymore, until one day he cornered me, and we actually talked about us and how compatible we were.

Can you believe it, a little girl in grade seven talking about compatibility? Anyway, we talked, and then I stopped running from him and started taking the bus with him, again. His friends were very nice to me, and he never forced anything on me. I liked him for that. Then, one day, we were going on the bus and he was rude to me. I felt disrespected in front of his friends, so I walked away and took another bus. I never spoke to him after that. Every time I would see him in school, I'd just walk away from him or just try my best not to ever run into him.

One day, his best friend saw me and my friend, Shanny, on the staircase before class, and he gave me a letter. This was my very first love letter. It was even typed up. I was like, *Man, this guy is smooth.* His family probably had money, because only people with money had a computer during those times, not to mention a printer. I couldn't believe it. I opened the letter and scanned it fast, because my friend wanted to read it too, but I just needed to be alone to take it in. Before I could fold it back up, I saw "I love you" at the bottom of it. My heart melted. I didn't know what to do. I just stood there and looked at those three words. It was even typed in a different font. I had to find him. I had to hug him or squeeze him or something. I knew the letter was an apology, so I told myself I needed to let him know that I accepted his apology.

As I said before, he was a few years older than me, so his classes were farther towards the back of the school than mine. I found him right after my last class, and we stood by his classroom door. He held my hand, and he spoke to me, so sweetly, softly, and gently. While he talked, all I could think about was that I needed this boy to hold me, but he never did. That was when I realized something was definitely weird about him. After that, we continued our 'no contact relationship.' No contact, as in he never touched me other than hold my hand, and he also never called me on the weekends. We probably talked on the phone five times maximum, if that much. But I wasn't complaining. I liked the idea of seeing him when I saw him. The situation eventually got old, and we just faded out.

Then, one Saturday afternoon, Davia's Auntie Dahlia, one of my mother's good friends, came by and asked my mother if I could go with them to Emancipation Park later on that day, and my mother said yes. Although I didn't have as many nice clothes or as much money as my friends in those days, I still liked hanging with them, and I didn't bother complaining about material things. I just wanted to have fun.

Although I didn't have enough money to go on the rides, I still enjoyed my night out, and I even saw some of my friends from Camperdown High that night. Seeing them was pretty cool, but I met someone who pretty much made the memory what it is. His name was Shane. Yup, another Shane. Because I always looked and acted older than my age, he thought I was actually fifteen, when I was only turning thirteen. He was turning seventeen. I was surprised when a little girl ran up to me and said, "Hey! I think my brother likes you."

I smiled and turned my back when he came over and started joking with Davia and me. He asked me my name and told me I was pretty. I said "Thanks," and continued to sit and stare out into space.

He said, "So yuh nah gimmie yuh numba?" (*Translation: So you're not going to give me your number?*)

I refused for a while until both his sisters, who were too cute to say no to, convinced me to give it to him, and so I did. Shane called that night. We laughed and talked. I wondered where he got so much credit (calling minutes) from, but I enjoyed his company on the phone anyway. He told me he went to Calabar High, a prestigious all boys' high school.

We met up at the bus park one day after school. We sat down and talked, and he bought me Burger King. Now, in those days, eating Burger King during school hours or on a weekday was a big deal to me and my friends. That meant you or your family must have some sort of money, because not everybody could afford Burger King during the week. Some of us were considered blessed to even be able to eat it on the weekends.

Before I continue this story, you must know that in Jamaica a thirteen-year-old is equivalent to a fifteen- or sixteen-year-old in North America. For the simple fact that once you start high school, you are exposed to a different environment due to being a teenager. As you know, that is the age a student starts high school in North America.

So I told Jhevante and Shanny about Shane the next day at school. I told them I would be meeting him at the bus park again that day. They both followed me to meet up with him. He went to the bank and pulled out some money and gave all my friends two hundred dollars each. They all loved him after that. Everyone wanted to come with me when I was meeting up with him. I had to lie and say I wasn't meeting him for the rest of the week, although I did. Shane was a sweetheart. He always made sure I was good, and he knew my family did not have much, and his family did. Plus, he was working part-time at his uncle's business place, so they had some change. I always questioned how wealthy his family was, though. It wasn't until one day when he invited me to meet his mother that I realized they actually did live a decent life. I went to his house in my uniform after school one day. On the way there, all I could think of was the beating I would get if my mother found out.

His house was a nice white and blue two-story house. He introduced me to his mother and his brother, and we watched TV in the living room for a little while, until we went to his room to watch more TV.

At least I can say with him we actually kissed. He barely even brushed me. He just made sure I was comfortable and fed. His mother was very nice, and she made sure I did not stay too long and that I went home before night fell. I never went back to his house, though, not because I didn't want to but because it just didn't happen. I hated the idea of walking with him in my uniform, and he understood. He wasn't rushing anything. Neither was I.

Shane always made me eat well, no matter what. Whenever I saw him, I was eating well, even though we only saw each other after school. He did the sweetest thing for me that I will never forget. It was Valentine's Day, and he got me a huge basket with a teddy bear and flowers. I don't think anyone understands the life I was living at such a young age, and it is not until now that I realize what was really going on. I opened up the basket right there in the bus park with my friends, and I obviously had to share up everything in it amongst us, because there was no way I was bringing it home to my mother's house.

Everyone got something out of the basket, but there was still more stuff left in there. I just brought it home to Mommy and told her I got it for her for Valentine's Day. Sorry, Mommy. She loved it, though. These, amongst many other nice things, were done by Shane. Unfortunately, I always felt like I never gave him as much as he gave me. And now I will never be able to give back to him the way I would like to because we lost contact. I don't think I will ever meet someone who is genuinely as nice as he was, and he took nothing back from me.

You see how funny life is? You will come across those people who seem to be draining everything you have in you, and then there will be those who you just can't understand why they have not even taken a little bit out of you… but that is just life.

Self-assessment: I tell the stories of these two guys because I want you to note in this chapter, as well as the previous one, the fact that at such a young age I somehow felt like I needed a male to validate me, or perhaps to complete me. This is a culture that young girls are being brought up in today. If you are following carefully, this all happened after my father left, and although I didn't live with my father, we spent enough time together. The question is why was a seventh grader rushing to be in a relationship? Why was this so important to me? I ask myself this question over and over again until this day. Was it because I was physically bigger and my hormones were at one hundred? Or perhaps I was a product of my environment.

Lesson:

~ *Don't stress over things you have no control over. Sometimes you must sit back, relax, and let life take its course.*

~ *"Let go and let God."*

The Emancipation Park

"A rare jewel in the heart of Kingston city, Emancipation Park is a refuge for many who seek solitude and a soothing ambience away from the hustle and bustle of daily living. It's an oasis where one can rejuvenate among its lush seven-acre landscape that symbolizes the legendary beauty of the island of Jamaica.

"Nature lovers can bask in the Park's scenery lined with tropical flowers and trees such as the majestic Royal Palm, its branches stretching outwards beckoning to the skies. Art lovers can appreciate the beautifully crafted 11ft. bronze sculpture *Redemption Song* by celebrated Jamaican artist Laura Facey that graces the ceremonial entrance of the park.

The opening of Emancipation Park in July 2002 is a significant milestone in the journey of our nation. The park was created to be a symbol of our freedom to hope, to excel and to be."
(www.emancipationpark.org)

Land of Opportunity 6

When I heard of the possibilities of moving to Canada, I was speechless. There were no words to describe the excitement. But the first day I stepped foot on this Promise Land, if I was able to walk on the ocean top back to 193½ Constant Spring Road, Kingston, Jamaica, I would.

The possibility of living in Canada obviously came through my father and his 'wife,' a lady I had no idea about until a few days before my set departure date. I mean, the man even got married without inviting his children to his wedding. How crazy is that?

Let's slow it down a bit. First of all, I've had a passport since grade five going into grade six, about a year and a half after my father left. Now, having a passport at that age was a huge deal for me. Why? Because home-girl got to collect her own money at Western Union now. My mother was usually the one to collect the money when my father would send it, but not after I got my passport. My passport was a valid I.D. and access to my cash.

Fredericka is not a woman that runs certain jokes. Even though she gave me the freedom of collecting my own money, I still had to bring back the receipt and every last penny. The journey to Western Union was a good walk from my house. I had to walk out of my lane, so I had to pass Ms. Sylvie, Ms. Peggy, and Ms. Phyllis. Not only that, I had to pass the little shop which was owned by Shu-Shu's aunt. This was the go-to shop where I got immediate service. It's sort of like a convenience store. Not a supermarket or a wholesale, but it was convenient enough to fulfill the immediate surroundings and last minute needs.

Quick side note: My mother was a very prideful woman, I don't know if you can tell yet, but trust me, she is. Despite the shop closest to us, I remember how my mother used to send us all the way down to another shop, which was at least a twenty-minute walk away from my house, just so our immediate neighbours wouldn't know what we were buying, especially if she was buying very small parcels of things, like a pound of flour and three pounds of chicken back.

Now, I don't know if you know how little a pound of flour is, but when times were rough, Mommy handled business, and we all got to eat from that one pound. Also, chicken back was not the most exquisite type of meat—more bones than meat—so folks hated when others knew that chicken back would be their dinner.

Now, back on task. Heading up to the Western Union, I had to pass the grounds where the boys in the community play soccer, although there was no grass. It was mostly concrete. Sometimes the girls would play netball or just hang out and gossip. This place was called Uppa Site. It was a power plant that was barred off with barbed wire, but it had some extra free land in front of it so we all took advantage of the space. Therefore, if I passed and saw a friend, I would have to stop and chat for a bit and get caught up on the latest Cassava Piece gossip, like who was dating who, the fresh teenage pregnancies, or who and who 'don't talk' and why. After passing Uppa Site, there were a few zinc-fenced yards and a navy blue painted shop called "Ms. Juan shop," which pretty much sold the same things as Shu-Shu's aunt's shop. After that was a drug dealer's house, who will remain nameless, although I doubt he is still alive. Ironically, across from him was a huge Seventh Day Adventist church with the sweetest hairy mango and guinep trees and, to guard those trees, a man who took care of and lived at the church. He owned a nice slingshot and was not afraid to use it. His name was Tiger. Tiger used to shoot at us for climbing the guinep tree. Now, I always followed a crowd that was older than me, or just a bunch of boys. But, trust me, if you can't run, don't you dare even think about trying to go pick a mango or guinep at Tiger's church. He will shoot you with that slingshot the minute he smells someone on his property. And he didn't care if your parent would come and complain, because he considered it private property, although it was on a completely open land. Tiger didn't care. He didn't want anyone picking his guineps or mangoes, even though he couldn't eat them all. He didn't mind them getting rotten and falling off the trees, just as long as none of the kids in the community got to pick them.

After Tiger's, there was Davia's house, and above that was her mother's bar. After passing her mother's bar and making a sharp left, there was one of my favourite places to be at these times, the supermarket on Khemlani Mart Plaza. Directly in front of the plaza was the main road, Constant Spring Road. Across the road was one of Jamaica's largest golf courses. However, I'd be staying on the plaza side. After passing the plaza, directly behind it was what we called Constant Spring Market. It's not a large market like the one most people would hear about that is located in downtown Kingston, but nevertheless it was a market. Behind the market were a lot of fresh water fish vendors, bars, a dress maker, and a shoe maker. Directly in front of the market, across the street, was a place called Discount Pharmacy. Although I have no idea why they called it Discount Pharmacy, because it was the most expensive pharmacy I've ever been in. A few steps past Discount Pharmacy was the plaza that housed the Western Union. This plaza had a KFC, Burger King, Subway, ice-cream place, Hi-Lo Supermarket, a gas station, a bank, Island Grill, Sugar and Spice—the best patty and pastry store—and, of course, Western Union.

With all these temptations in one plaza, my mother still expected me to bring her back every penny. This was more difficult than I could have handled most times, but I'd rather starve than take a beating from my mother. So, you guessed it, I always brought back every penny until I started feeling liberated. Once I hit high school and the beatings were less, I took full advantage of my freedom.

My father only sent money twice a month, if I was lucky. My school fees were high, bus fare was high, and lunch money was another story. Although Mommy made it work, she never hesitated to remind me of how good of a kid I was, because I never pressured her. I always took what I got and was satisfied with it. You would think that by collecting my own money I would want to spend it in abundance, especially to show off when I was passing by everyone with my passport and Western Union slip, letting them know I got money. But nope, not me. I gave it all, because now that I had full access to it I realized that it wasn't much. Looking back now, I wonder how she made it work. If you were to ask her now she would say, "We just made it work."

There were days I went to school with just bus fare because I had to take two, sometimes three, buses, and after bus fare, there was just not enough for lunch money for the whole week. I remember days when I couldn't wait to go home because I knew Mommy wouldn't let us go to bed without food.

There were times when I had to ask my closest school friend for some of his lunch, too. I will never forget Jhevantee Scott, who was a boy taller than me, medium build, with a nice boxed shaped hairline, full lips, and full, bright black eyes. We attended the same primary school, and out of all the sixth graders, we were the only two who passed for the same high school. So, you guessed it, we stuck together. If there were days he didn't have food, he would take some of mine, and if there were days I didn't have, I took some of his. Sometimes we even ripped the lunch box plates in half, ripped a corner of the plate to use it as spoon, and we shared our lunch like it was nobody's business. We didn't care, we were still happy. We grew very close a little bit before our GSAT results came out because we had mutual friends. Plus we were both Capricorns.

After spending almost a year at Camperdown High School, my two siblings and I got the news in the beginning of June that our visas would soon be ready. The news couldn't come to me any sooner. In Jamaica, they have a saying that goes "Yuh glad bag buss" (*Translation: Your glad bag is broken.*) It's something people would say when you are extremely happy about something and you start to go a little crazy. So, yeah, when I got the news my glad bag did buss. Not only because it was around exam time and this meant I could have just slacked off because I was going to be migrating out of the country, but also because a few days after I got the news, Jhevantee also got the news that he would also be flying out to a foreign country that summer to go visit his father who lived in Florida. Although I was migrating for good and he was just visiting, we were happy for each other, nonetheless. It was just that he couldn't slack off with the exams like I could. Although, generally, he took his education seriously.

My anticipation grew greater. Back in Jamaica, moving to a foreign country was a big deal. The people and the television told you that it is where all the stars lived; everyone wanted to be there. Food was never a problem—though, let me be the first to say that Scarborough, Ontario, Canada was the first place I felt a real headache type of hunger. I figured I could go on the bed with my shoes, because I would probably always be wearing a new pair. I could wear regular clothes to school and not a uniform. The place would always be clean. I would be living in a house with a driveway, and when I turned sixteen, I could start driving my own car, which I probably would get on my sweet sixteen. Everything would just be better there. I could go on and on about this façade.

I actually started building a concept of what my Canadian house would look like. I mean the whole thing. I took some ideas from my favourite TV shows, and I drew out a whole concept in my head. I pictured an orange-ish brown brick exterior. There would be a well-groomed, lush, green lawn, and when we pulled up to the driveway, there would be two cars, because my sister was over sixteen and should be able to drive. The house would have an open concept kitchen; as I entered, I could see all the kitchen appliances. There would be a silver or black fridge, where we would hang our report cards and activities' reminders. There would be a living room that was clean and spacious with a large flat screen TV, and couches would be there, too. Our rooms would be upstairs. I thought maybe my brother would have his own, and Tee and I would share, although I was hoping we wouldn't have to. So, in my mind, I added two separate beds and closets to our room.

I couldn't even believe I was thinking about closets back in Jamaica. Of course, half of my wardrobe was my big sister's hand-me-downs, because her father's side of the family lived in America and would always send her nice things that were in style. Our kitchen was sort of a part of my brother's room, and the dishes had to be washed in a pail under a pipe outside the back of our house. My big sister and I shared a room. My mother had hers, and we had a tiny living room. Now, this house to me was luxury compared to the board house we used to live in during my earlier years. At the tenement yard, the shower and toilet were outside, and there was only one for everybody in the yard to use. In fact, it was barely a bathroom. It was just a toilet beside a concrete wall, where they made an impromptu hose as a shower and barred it around with some zinc, and that is where we showered. However, the best part about a tenement yard is that all the kids would link up by just stepping outside their doors. I could have literally walked from my door right into someone else's house within a few steps. Or we would just go to the open space in the yard where we would play games like dandy-shandy, hopscotch, skipping, Chinese-skip, ring games, marbles, and hide-and-seek.

However, thank God, Mommy Fredericka worked two jobs tirelessly as a domestic and Free Zone factory worker to get us out of there and build her own concrete house down the road beside Ms. Sylvie. So, believe me when I tell you that when I heard about indoor showers, hot water, and a nice kitchen with food in abundance, I was like, *Whoa! Let's start packing right now. I'm ready to roll out.*

At this point, I was so looking forward to landing in Canada that at night I could barely sleep, especially as the days got closer. I had to leave my mother and go stay with one of my stepmothers because she, along with my big sister, Tammy, handled all our documentations and was travelling up and down to get things done. Tee and Damion's mother was not present in our lives, and they lived in the country with my grandmother. Plus, she lived closer to the airport, so Tee, Damion, and I had to meet up there and go to the airport from there.

Our flight was an early morning flight, so we were at my stepmom's place like two days ahead of time. That is when I found out that it would only be Damion and I who would be leaving that day. There were some issues with Tee's ticket. To be honest, at the time, I didn't really care about the issue as long as it had nothing to do with me not leaving, because, trust me, all those exams that I slacked off on Mommy would not be happy if she found out. So, as long as the problem had nothing to do with me, my glad bag was buss, and I was on an all-time high. I was very anxious, though I played it cool.

The morning finally arrived. I don't remember even sleeping that night. All I know was that my stepmother, Damion, and I were in the Norman Manley airport with our suitcases. My mother, my big sister, and the stepdad I hated were also there. I don't even know why she brought him along, but I was too happy to care.

The problems started right away in the airport, before we even took off. We were there about two hours before our flight was to leave, when we learned that because we were underage we needed to pay some sort of money for the flight attendants to take care of us and to take us through customs and to my father safely. Now, no one that was with us at the time had that sort of money on them, so we called my father and told him the news. Although he was very upset that none of the adults there had the money, he somehow called a friend who lived close by to loan us the money. Oh, by the way, did I tell you that my father was a taxi driver in Jamaica, with two cars before he moved to Canada? Well, yeah, I thought you should know he was.

I saw a sign of relief wash over my mother's face when my father's friend came through with the money. My mother is a hard-core Jamaican woman, as you may already know, so she didn't really cry when we were leaving. She just said things like, "Look out for your siblings up there. Make sure you never put your panty in no washing machine; use your hand to wash those. Keep your surroundings clean. Remember your manners, because it look like foreign pickney don't have any. Follow the rules, and don't stress out your father. Call me as soon as you reach, and if you have a stepmother when you go up there, make sure you respect her." Dad knew Mommy was a no B.S. kind of woman. Unlike the others, she never took any talk from him. She was the boss lady…at least that is what I think.

We got on the plane, and as soon as it took off, Damion and I both fell asleep. I just wanted to wake up in Canada. I was a nervous wreck. I have no idea how I even fell asleep in the first place. This black man dressed in a white, short-sleeved shirt with a blue, red, and yellow tie, blue pants, and black shoes escorted us off the plane and straight through the airport customs and all that. Then he led us to my father, his cousin, Nadine, her husband, Tommy, and Cousin Mark.

I greeted my father first, who was wearing a fresh braid-up, fresh white tee, blue jeans, and some white and blue Nikes, with the biggest hugs known to man, and he reciprocated the gesture then introduced us to everyone.

We exited the airport, where there were two cars, and then I thought back to my mental picture and confirmed the two cars in there. I hopped in a blue Honda Civic with my father and Nadine. Damion hopped into a nice looking black sleek Acura with Mark and Tommy. I was awestruck. I was like, *Oh, man! This is it! I'm finally in paradise!* However, that feeling didn't last very long.

Remember how I said I would go right back to Cassava Piece if I could? Yeah, right then would have been a good time. About fifteen minutes outside of the airport, the car that I was in got a busted tire, and we had to pull over off the highway. The thing ripped off right down to the rim! It was not just a flat tire or something simple; we were completely rimmed. Luckily, Dad had a spare tire in the back, and he was an auto body worker, so I knew he could fix it. But, trust me, that shit was scary, especially for my first few minutes in Canada.

I thought to myself, *Why did it have to happen to my car, right now?* Not that I would want it to happen to the car my brother was in, I just wanted to know 'why me?'

Looking back now, this may have been a sign that I would not have much luck in this country. The car was back on the road, and I couldn't wait to get to our house. But before we got to our house, my father decided he didn't like the sandals I was wearing, and the insults towards my mother started there. He acted like he sent a ton of money, and she did nothing with it, when in fact, the money started coming in my name. I realized it was next to nothing that he was sending anyway, but yet we thanked God that he at least sent something.

We went to a shoe store called Si Vous Play, and I picked up about three different pairs of shoes off the wall. With so much to choose from, I felt like I was in sneaker heaven. I told my dad that these were what I wanted, not thinking that he would have a problem with it, because when he visited Jamaica once from Canada he gave me almost anything I asked for.

But instead he said, "No, Rudy, put those back," Then he led me to what was labelled as a "Sale" rack.

I picked out a pink and white G-Unit Reebok sneaker. Damion picked out a blue and white Puma-looking Nike, and that was all we got that day. After our purchases, we finally arrived at a tall cream building marked 126 with too many floors to count. I'd never seen anything quite like it, especially with people living in it. I mean, there were some buildings in Half Way Tree, Kingston's capital, that were tall, but they only housed businesses. We would only see workers coming out of them between the hours of nine-to-five. I've never actually stepped foot in one, but I heard they had the best air conditioning systems, especially for a place as hot as Jamaica.

We were then told to take our stuff out of the car. Yup, we were home. No lush green lawn and no two-car driveway. This was obviously not what I envisioned, but I was still curious to see what the inside looked like. We entered the building with a small silver key that my dad used at the front door. We took a couple steps and were facing what looked like three stainless steel silver doors with a button in the middle. We pressed the button and waited for a few seconds before one slowly opened. Yes, you guessed it, they were elevators. *Canadian living was pretty cool*, I thought, *we will be using an elevator every day!* Coming from a place where we walked to do almost everything, I was excited and knew that I could get used to this. We exited the elevator on the seventh floor, made a sharp left, took approximately five steps, and stopped at door number 709. We opened it and entered.

The first thing I noticed was the smell of the place. It was a weird smell, not bad though, but weird like nothing I had ever smelled before. The place was not an open concept, not spacious, definitely not, but anyhow, it was still nice to me. It had a living room with a computer, couches, and a TV—not a flat screen, but it would do. The kitchen had counters, cupboards, a white stove, a microwave, and a refrigerator. I thought to myself, *Well, this place is actually fully decked out. I sure could get used to this.*

We were then led to our room by my dad, while my cousins helped themselves to drinks and smokes on an outside piece of the apartment that I was told was called a balcony. The room had a nice-sized cream and gold bed-set with a dresser, two bedside tables, and a closet, plus an extra bed. Yes, all three of us would be sleeping in the same room. I still really had no complaints, but I was very sceptical. The place looked nothing like I had envisioned and nothing like what my father had promised us.

The first thing I did was take a shower. There was hot and cold water, and you got to set it to your liking. I had fun in that shower. Although in my mom's house there was an indoor shower, there definitely wasn't any hot water. When I got out of the shower and got dressed, the house had more people than when I had gotten in. My father had invited a few friends over to meet and greet us. They hugged and welcomed us. They smoked, drank, laughed, and talked until the sun was going down. My dad asked us if we wanted something to eat. We said yes, and he ordered pizzas and wings. Man, we had a feast! I thought to myself, *Maybe this Canada thing is cool, you know?*

I still couldn't see the reality of what was about to hit. I couldn't wait to see what was in store for us the next day, because I was enjoying everything so far. We went to bed that night peacefully, although I can't quite recall when I slipped off into sleep and if everyone was even gone yet. I slept well.

Finally, morning came, and the sun hit my face through the white blinds that hung in front of the window in our room. My brother was also up around the same time. We did our usual morning routine—brushed our teeth, showered, and headed to the living room area to see what cool shows they had on the TV. Most importantly, we wanted to know what we would have for breakfast. That morning we shared a bit of small talk with my father about how things were in Jamaica, who was doing what, and so on. This same routine went on for about three days. We woke up, did our routine, ate breakfast, brought Pops up to speed on Jamaica, and had occasional visits from new faces.

Then, my sister arrived. Damion, my pops, Cousin Nadine, and I went to pick her up from the airport as well. When she got to the house and was settled in, we started going out with my pops to visit different people who would give us money and welcome us. We opened bank accounts, received our health cards, were given our social security numbers, and got up to speed with all that was necessary to survive in this country. Luckily, it was summertime, and we got to do those things in the warmth.

The weeks flew by. Nadine had three kids—two girls and a boy who were younger than my siblings and me. Another cousin of ours, Orvillle, also had three kids—three boys. So we had company at all the impromptu apartment barbeques that were held by my pops and his friends.

During these times, I discovered a lot about Canada and my pops. I discovered that he had multiple women, was an excessive drinker, and smoked weed. He also sold weed. Therefore, when we had visitors on a semi-regular basis, they weren't only coming to welcome us, they were also coming to make their purchases. I noticed this when the faces started becoming familiar. That was now my reality. *What am I supposed to do?*

As a child, you just go wherever they put you, no complaints and no arguments. I even thought that we would've been living with our pops and his wife. I remember one day, during back to school time, we were all signing up for school with Nadine. Afterwards, my pops tried to take us shopping when he got home from work that day. You wouldn't believe where the man took us. He took us to Goodwill, and not the nice Goodwill stores that are cool now because thrifting is trendy, but the Goodwill where people dump their old clothes. As if sensing and speaking something telepathically, all three of us stood there and said nothing. We didn't even explore the racks. After noticing our sadness, he had the nerve to ask us if we didn't see anything we liked. Up to this day, my siblings and I laugh at that encounter.

When we got back to the apartment, he started telling us how difficult it is to live in a country like this. He reminded us that this place was no bed of roses. I asked him what he was talking about, and he began to tell the story about how his wife kicked him out a few months after he arrived in Canada. He said she was stingy with food and that she tried to encourage him to forget his kids.

I said to myself, *Damn! If this story is true, I'm glad I didn't meet her.* One thing about my pops, when it came down to food, he was never stingy. He fed everyone. The younger kids loved him because he would always make sure they were fed and happy.

Lesson:

~ No matter what they tell you, present to you, or promise you, always want to see for yourself. Always read the fine print.

7 Family Issues and Physical Abuse

My brother, Damion, and I were only a month apart. He was older, so he ended up going to high school, and was placed in the ninth grade. I ended up in middle school, in the eighth grade. So, yeah, we were split in two, and the black sheep walked to school alone, while the other two took the bus together. Not that I was sweating the idea, I was just hoping I had someone familiar to roll with me in school, you know?

On my first day in middle school, I was sitting in the office waiting to be placed in my class. A short, light-skinned girl came up to me and said, "Hey, are you new from Jamaica?"

"Yes," I replied.

"Ok, cool!" she said in a friendly manner. "Come, let me show you around. My dad is from Jamaica too, and my mom is white."

"I'm just waiting to get to my class. I never been in the classroom yet," I answered in a semi-patois dialect. I mean, I went to a prestigious high school in Jamaica, and I had to know how to speak proper English. Where that was concerned, I wasn't worried. I knew I would catch on to their accent, sooner or later. Naturally, a fish can only reflect the water it's been swimming in.

"Miss J, what class is she in? I can take her?" she asked the secretary. I wasn't paying much attention to the answer she got, but apparently, I was in her class.

She smiled her perfectly white teeth at me and said, "My name is Jenel. Come on, you're in my class. Pick up your bag and let's go!"

As soon as we walked out of the office, a two door room was facing us, and she told me that was the cafeteria, which is where we would be having our lunch. She explained everything about the school that she thought I needed to know, and more. From the recess area, the gym, woodshop class, music class, our lockers, and finally our homeroom. I nodded and smiled.

"Hey, yo Reem! This is Tasheka. She is fresh from Jamaica!" she called out to a short, slim, beautiful, black-curly-haired, dark-skinned girl. She looked like the Indians I would see in Jamaica. I learned that day that Reem was from Ethiopia.

Our homeroom class was in the back of a library, and our teacher was a short and stubby white man whose lips always seemed to be chapped. That class was where we would start and end our days for as long as we went to John McCrae Senior Public School. The class was very multi-cultural. It had the Whites, Sri-Lankans, Pakistanis, Chinese, Japanese, Tamils, and born Canadians of different backgrounds. These people were from places I had never heard of in my life, and some of them even spoke funny. I wondered if that's what they said about me.

I went to school the next few weeks, still trying to adjust to my new lifestyle and new environment. I was placed in the clarinet section in music class. Jenel made sure I sat beside her in computer class. English wasn't so bad, because it was the homeroom teacher who also taught us English. I already hated math, so you know how that goes. I started memorizing how to get to my classes, and the combination to my locker.

Jenel introduced me to some of the other kids. I thought to myself, *Man, this girl knows everyone.* That was only a thought, until I realized Jenel was one of the big dogs. I mean, she was one of the popular, cool kids in the school. I was so thankful, and I couldn't believe how lucky I was to have her as a friend.

Most of the people she introduced me to usually looked at me funny. You could see the judgment in their eyes. They judged my clothes, my shoes, my hair, and even my looks. I was just this tall eighth grade girl, who was taller than most of the girls in my class, dark-skinned, with not very long hair. Like Jenel and some of the others, I didn't have the Jordan's or the cool clothes they had. I was just regular old me, trying to get some good grades in class. I realized afterward that most of the cool kids didn't even get good grades, but they had the most fly gear and made fun of those who didn't. Even one of my Cousin Orville's kids went to that school and was in the same class as me, but he barely acknowledged me.

Months were going by, and winter was in full swing. We had already seen our first snowfall. We feared our pops, and the house had a set routine now. My father would leave our lunch money on the table the night before when he went to bed. We woke up, showered, got dressed, and went to school, while Pops went to work his nine-to-five. After school, someone had to be home to sell the weed, and Damion and Tee were obviously closer than I was. This was all crazy to me. I had to wake myself up in the mornings, and that was a difficult task, in and of itself, having come from Jamaica, where my mother or my big sister woke me up every morning for school. It took some getting used to. The lunch money wasn't enough, especially for my brother and sister who were taking the bus, but we never dared to complain about it.

By then we learned how to weigh the weed. It was 3.5g, which is a half a quarter, for $30. And some people, depending on who it was and whether they had their own scales or not, got more or less. My pops would tell us that if he didn't call and tell us that someone was coming, we should never let them in, and always make sure to check the peephole, never let in any strange faces, and don't bring friends from school over without asking him first.

Back when we used to visit our dad's house in Jamaica, I used to get B+'s and up. He made a comment once that I was his star child. My siblings resented me for that for years. I mean, I had nothing to do with his comment; I was just young and doing what I needed to do as a kid.

As time went by in Canada, I would always get in trouble with my pops. Whether it was not cleaning the bathroom on time, or not cleaning it enough, or not doing the dishes. There was always something, and getting into trouble with my pops wasn't just a simple argument. It travelled the world to all the members of our family, and he humiliated me as much as he could. I was intimidated for years by a tall, thick, black man with braids and gold teeth—a man whom I call Daddy.

When it was report card time, I would always get good grades, but because I would argue with the teacher, mostly about some of the grades I thought were unfair, my father would only see the comments section and not the grades. So he would still get at me. I got into more trouble those first few years than any other of his children. I was even threatened to be sent home on several occasions. One day, Pops came home early. He said there was a Bell Canada bill on the table, and we should cross off all the numbers on it that were ours. Let me tell you, this bill came up to $1,071.67. We were all shitting bricks. We would usually hideout in our rooms when my father came home, but this day was something different. We just thought we were going to be sent home for sure. He would always tell us to buy calling cards if we wanted to call Jamaica, and not use the house phone. We barely had enough lunch money much less any to buy calling cards. Plus, we were too scared of him to ask him to buy us cards. So, we checked off our numbers and, you guessed it, mine was the most, coming in first with $708.03. Tee was second up with $292.60. Damion was in last place with a meagre $71.04.

I wanted to call my mother almost every day, so most of my calls were to her. After that, I had it bad for months, if not years, hearing about this phone bill. I was so close to being sent home that family members from all over the world called to scold me. My pops even went as far as making me feel bad by calling out my brother and sister to sit and talk in the living room with him while I stayed in the room by myself. I spent weeks trying to regain his approval to no avail. Tee seemed to enjoy this episode the most, not so much Damion because he just didn't really care for the whole charade.

Shit really hit the fan when one day at school, Jenel and I were in class at last period and were chatting away about something, when my cousin, Orville, came over to me and said, "Yo, hold this iPod down for me. Take it home, and then bring it back tomorrow." I was cool with it. *I could use an iPod in that house right now.* I was amped, and I had the iPod for about a day or so, when a girl in my class said her iPod was missing and that she had it in class that day at that exact time. She swore that she saw Orville take the iPod, but when the teacher asked if anyone saw the iPod in class, I kept my mouth shut. I learned in that class that no one ever snitches, so I said nothing.

They called Orville down to the principal's office and apparently threatened to suspend him for ten days if he didn't come up with the iPod. Then, would you believe it? Orville told the principal that I stole the iPod! Well, you better believe it, because he did. They called me down, and since he had already snitched, I gave up the iPod. They held me in the office that evening and called my pops to come pick me up. Then, they explained the whole story to him, obviously saying that I was to be suspended for ten days because I had stolen someone's iPod.

Just as I was getting cut some slack for the phone bill, that happened. I was literally living in hell for a few months. I was yelled at, cussed at, and ridiculed by my pops constantly. As bad as I had to deal with my father, there came times when I had to deal with my sister, who just simply treated me bad for no reason. She seemed to find joy in making me suffer. She always thought I was my father's favourite kid and that he loved me the most. Interestingly enough, in our first few months in Canada, Pops sat us down and told us that she was his eldest child. He said he had to show her more love than us sometimes because she is a female and she never grew up with him or her mother, so he didn't want her going out and looking elsewhere for love. I remember a situation where something happened in the house, and my father insisted that I was the one who did it. He went as far as to say that Tee would never lie and that I am the liar like my mother.

My sister barely even did my hair anymore, and she was a hair dresser by nature. I had to beg and hope she was in a good mood to do my hair. I was laughed at and even ridiculed when I went to school with my ponytail to the back, because that was all I knew how to do. I could go on and on about scenarios of the bad treatment I received, simply because, in my opinion, I had a different mother than her and my brother.

I'm writing this now, not to throw shade at my sister, because we are grown now and hopefully past that stage. I even tried to explain to her once how badly she treated me, and she gave a half-ass apology, which nonetheless was an apology, and I appreciated it.

One day, I came home from school first and was on the computer, when Tee came through the door and demanded that she needed the computer. Now, before I tell you this story, let me say that my sister was a very rough and bitter person in my opinion, but she managed to hide it, when necessary, with a pretty little smile and a soft, baby voice used to manipulate people into thinking she was a goody two shoes, especially the men in her life. This is just my personal observation over the years.

When she demanded the computer, I gave it to her. Later on that day, she seemed to be having trouble with the computer. Since we came to Canada, I was pretty much the computer go-to person, only because I had done computer classes in school in Jamaica. I knew my way around the thing. She called out to me and asked for my help, and I came to help. At that age, I was struggling to be liked or loved or whatever you want to call it, by my father and my sister, whenever I was home. And at school, I was struggling to be liked by my then peers as well, so I did whatever I could, when I was able.

Fixing the computer issue took much longer than expected, and by the time the issue was about to be fixed, Pops walked in. He walked by our room, and Tee must've looked sad to him, so he asked what was wrong. And her response, as vividly as I remember was, "Mi tell Rudy seh mi want use the computer and from shi come from school she deh pon it." (*Translation: I told Rudy I needed to use the computer, but since she got home from school she's been on it.*) I was like, *Whaaat?* I couldn't believe she said that. I was so shocked. Then Pops came and started cussing at me, once again, saying how I loved the computer too much, blah, blah, blah. I just got up and went to my room. Tee tortured and ignored me for days in the house. We slept in the same bed, and she would toss and turn or screw up her face, and so forth.

A few months later, we moved into a bigger apartment, with Tee and me in one room, Damion had his own room, and my pops had his. One night, Damion came into our room, and all three of us were lying in the bed. Out of nowhere, Tee and Damion started to fight. I mean like kicking and slapping over me while I laid in the midst of it all. I finally developed the courage to break it up, when Tee gave me the slap of my life. I heard a soft ringing tone in my ears, followed by a sting to my skin that night.

I explained to Pops what happened, and he just said, "No fighting," and went back to his bed. Yes, that hurt. It really cut me deep. But, at that age, after a while, when things like that happened, time helped the memory fade a bit, and I just kept moving forward. I had this sort of attitude because I had a lot of love on my mother's side of the family. Looking back at it now, it sort of balanced out a lot of what was in me. Thank God I have a lot of love in me.

With all that love, as I grew older, I learned to overlook certain things. Although, even to this day, people may say I am too nice, too forgiving, and give too much of myself to people. I can't say that I'd be the productive member of society that I am today without love. I might've been the extreme opposite. Maybe I would have had a selfish and counter-productive mindset that millions of my peers around the world have right now. I've been through many stages of poverty and being ridiculed because of my life situation, but at the same time, I can't say that there is anything that has made me into the young woman I am today as much as my past situation. Being with Fredericka, big sis Tammy, and bro Jamar in Jamaica helped me. And though we had our internal issues related to frustrations that built up because we didn't have much, we were a unit.

To me, at the time, it didn't really affect my psyche, because I knew that, nonetheless, I was loved and cared for deeply by my little Jamaican family. I will never forget the times when my mother lost her job, and Tammy, who had my nephew, still fed and took care of us as if she was the mother in the family. She never complained. Tammy did it genuinely and gracefully. We were survivors.

As I get older and reflect on the times that shaped my opinion of the world, I can't help but think back to the first time I was beaten badly by my father for absolutely no reason, except that he was intoxicated and paranoid. Now, when you hear me talk about being beaten by my mother, I'm not talking about a beating like this. My mother's beatings were solely for disciplinary actions with a belt, and when your name is Rudy in Jamaica, as good as your grades were, you still needed some sort of discipline.

On this particular night, the night of my sister's eighteenth birthday, Pops had a party for her in an empty apartment a few floors up on our building. A few days before the party, I sold fifty dollars worth of weed to a guy from across the street that my pops sent to me. Kim, a cousin of ours, came to visit us from New York, so she was at the party, as well as Jenel and a couple of my other friends from school. Jenel and I were coming from downstairs when Pops greeted me with a slap in my chest. Pow!

As soon as I entered the apartment I asked, "What did I do?"

He said, "Didn't I tell you guys not to come back upstairs? Wah di f**k uno a do up here?" (*Translation: What the f**k are you doing up here?*)

Confused, I asked, "What are you talking ab—" Before I could finish my sentence, Damion came around the corner, and my pops gave him a kick in his ass. We all ran back to the elevator and went straight to our room.

Damion, Jenel, and I were downstairs trying to figure out what was going on. Apparently, the fifty dollars that the guy from downstairs gave me that night was fake. He showed up at the party, and for some reason, my father thought the guy and his friends were coming to get him because he had told some of his friends that the guy had given me the fake money.

After a few minutes of us talking in the room, we heard the front door slam and Pops yelling. We didn't move. Then he came in the room wearing his dress pants, white shirt, and square-front dress shoes. The shoes landed right in my chest with the first kick. I held on to the wall to break my fall. In my face was the second, third, and fourth kick. I stood up with a straight face after each one.

There was a curling iron on the bed beside us, about as round as the circumference of your thumb to your middle finger, about three centimetres open. He gave me about five blows to the head with it, and I stood straight without tears. I just couldn't cry. I felt every hit, but I just couldn't. He ended with two more kicks, and then headed in my brother's direction, who ran away as he was coming at him. My brother managed to get about three kicks to his buttocks.

I looked over at Jenel and saw tears in her eyes. She kept asking if I was okay, and my answer remained "Yes," just "yes." Then we heard a loud scream. It was Tee's cry. Apparently, he had kicked her right above her vagina.

A couple of his friends started holding on to him, telling him to stop. Before we knew it, the night was extremely late. All the party guests were gone, and we were headed to a motel. Pops said we would be sleeping there for the night "in case the boys" came after him." No one was even looking for or cared about him.

Jenel, Kim, Tee, Damion, and I slept in the hotel that night. Then he came to pick us up in the morning and brought us back to our same house and same old regular living, with no harassment from anyone.

I never understood how you can love someone and hurt them that much. How can someone cause so much pain and say they loved you? I could never and will never get it. I mean, the pain I endured from this man was often unbearable. I even considered ending my life because of the pain.

With that being said, substance abuse, in any capacity, is not cool at all. A man that I knew to be caring, gentle, and understanding to his children became a monster. I didn't know who he was anymore, because of him drinking too much alcohol and smoking too much weed. It became more difficult when he didn't think he had a drinking problem or that weed was even a drug.

I've just listed three ongoing problems within our community that we fail to give attention to—suicide, alcoholism, and "weedism." Don't get me wrong, I am not shedding light on these situations because I hate my siblings or my father. In fact, I love my family; I love both sides unconditionally. I was just nurtured differently by one side than the other. Nonetheless, I love them both. My siblings and I still fallout, butt heads, and disagree occasionally, but I love them all the same. When I am around my siblings or my family, for that matter, a feeling of pure bliss comes to me. Up to this day, I still hate watching movies without Damion. Whenever we watched movies, we shared silly commentaries, and it's just different from watching movies with anyone else. Others just wouldn't understand our way of doing it; our connection is just indescribable.

I love the idea of family, like the whole unit concept of it. I can't wait to have my own family and nurture it the way I was nurtured by my mother, big sister, Tammy, and big brother, Jamar. I promise to make sure that they know how important it is to stick together, no matter the circumstance or situation. It is important that you remain a unit.

As you already know, Tammy has an amazing son, Rushane. Damion now has an adorable daughter, Jayda, and Tee has the most handsome son, Jairdan. When I see my siblings' children, my soul smiles. I love all my family; I'm just not as close as I'd like to be with them all the time. I would actually fight for my family in spirit and in truth. I am a warrior by nature—a prayer warrior, a spiritual warrior, and a physical and mental warrior. My family is a part of me, whether they choose to be or not. It's crazy how my mother has the same warrior spirit, but it doesn't cloud her judgment as a parent. She will fight for me and then discipline me at the same time.

I remember one time in primary school another kid and I got into it. Even though I was wrong, Mommy came and stood up for me in front of everyone, but when I got home I got a beating and a warning never to let it happen again or disgrace our family like that, again. Therefore, when there is conflict between my siblings and me, I don't hold it against them. I've endured pains and regrets about what happened, but that's life. You go through shit and keep it moving.

As you continue to read this book, please understand that I haven't created it to tell any lies or cause any pain. Even though my words may cause some damage, please remember it is all from my perspective, and I am rightfully entitled to that. I am here to share my reality and truth, which may not be the same as theirs. I hope that others who may be struggling right now will see my story as a testimony. There is good, even in the worst of people. In choosing to share my truth, it becomes a part of my healing process. Shedding light on these things will take them out of the darkness and give hope to not give up.

Whatever you are feeling, get it out, speak it, cry about it, or tell somebody. You need to heal from whatever it is that causes you pain and get beyond it. Once you have completed the healing process, you will be able to love selflessly and never give others the opportunity to dictate how you live or love.

> # Lesson:
> ~ I've learned over the years that children model and take a lot from the people who have been around them the most or who are connected to them the most. We absorb things in ways which we don't even see sometimes, but we do anyways. Trust me, I do it, too. Fredericka is the type of woman who is very prideful and has a very hard time expressing her weaknesses. I've also come to realize that I am the same. After a while, I've also grasped that the adults that Tee and Damion grew up around were also convinced that my pops loved me more and gave me more money than he did them. That was far from the truth, but somehow those types of false beliefs rubbed off on my brother and sister. Folks, please never forget the importance of family and maintaining the unit you were born into. No matter what, blood is blood.

A Note to Parents/Adults:

Remember, if you have addiction problems, it is likely that the people around you will be able to identify the problems before you do. Therefore, if they keep telling you that you have a problem, do not be afraid to seek help. Addictions can permanently damage your relationships with family and loved ones.

To Jamaicans:

Yes, weed is a drug! It has dangerous chemicals in it. The addiction to weed can become worse when mixed with nicotine or alcohol on a regular basis.

8 Love and Healing

Speaking of healing from things through speaking out about them, I'm about to share with you a situation that I was especially glad I was able to heal from.

One summer day, a cousin of mine brought over a tall, dark, slender, and handsome friend who was wearing a white t-shirt, greyish-bluish denim pants that were a bit too baggy, and a black and white pair of Nikes. Apparently, my cousin, Tee, and Damion knew this young man from Jamaica, because when he visited Jamaica he visited their area a few times.

I'm not too sure how we began talking that day, but I knew he told Tee that he liked me and that he was almost positive he saw me at their house in Jamaica before. I thought his face looked quite familiar, but it was nothing serious. We're going to call him "Daniel" for writing purposes. Now, Daniel and I started talking on the phone constantly since that day, and we grew to like each other. When Tee, Damion, and I would go out on weekends, he would come all the way from the West to the East to meet up with us and take me to the movies, or we would all just hangout along with two of his friends.

One evening while he waited for our bus with us at the subway station, he called me over to a corner behind a corridor and placed his lips on mine gently, exploring my top and bottom lips, and then started exploring the inside of my mouth with his tongue for a very long time. I felt things running up and down my spine and tingles in my stomach and body. I had never felt anything quite like it. I was weak to my knees. I forgot where I was, and I even forgot that outside of that kiss the world existed. To me, at the time, this was magical. This was a kiss I would never be able to forget. It was my first, real, deep kiss that alerted my whole body. At some point, although it was a difficult thing to do, we broke it off. I went on my bus, and he went on the train. I thought about this kiss for hours, days, and even months. I called him as soon as I got home, and we talked until he got into his place.

We spent hours on the phone every day, from sun down to sun up. He would call me during his work breaks, and any other free time he had, we would be on the phone. We talked about the kiss constantly and how magical it felt, like nothing we had ever felt before. He would come on weekends when he could with my cousin, and when my dad would leave the house or go to the bathroom, we would steal small kisses from each other on the balcony. We took a risk with my father that could have had both of us killed. I can't believe I even did that. We were so good together that my friends and cousins wished they had a boyfriend like Daniel.

He shared with me that he went to Jamaica at a young age to visit when he got a girl pregnant, and although he and the girl were no longer together, he took care of his daughter. It was then that I knew I should have left that situation, because I was just too young to be with a young man who had a child. I should have never entertained the idea at such a young age. It is times like this when I hate the fact that I was so mature and acted older than I actually was. Hence, I got involved in a situation that was not intended for a young lady my age. But I was in love, and nothing he did up to that point could have made me hate him. I loved him, and he loved me just the same, as far as I was concerned.

Summer was rolling on by, and we would still talk so much on the phone that my father banned me from the phone. That didn't stop me. Sometimes Tee would hog the phone, but that didn't stop me. Even at one point, my father actually broke our house phone because I forgot to put it on silent one night, and Daniel called about three times after midnight because he was working late and yup, you guessed it, that didn't stop me! It got to the point where Daniel even bought me my own cell phone that I hid from my pops and agreed to pay the bill. I was so happy because I knew my father would have never bought me one, especially with how he thought I loved the phone too much.

This is just a simple example that shows you that no matter how strict parents are and how much they shelter their children from certain things, the kids will do what they want or what they aren't supposed to do at some point. What is supposed to happen will happen, whether you like it or not. This doesn't mean you should let your children run wild. It just means you should keep an open line of communication. Don't sugar-coat the truth or the real world; tell your children what it is in addition to what may or may not happen to them if they make certain decisions. Do not try to instil a parental fear in them. It won't work. They will rebel any chance they get, just like Tammy did when my mother finally let her out.

A month had passed by during our relationship. Daniel was working so much, because he worked at the same place as his father and was not able to miss work. So we didn't see each other for a whole month, and that is when we had our very first argument. I missed him and didn't know how to deal with it, so we argued about it. I told him he was selfish and that he was probably seeing someone else for sex. He was so upset about those accusations, especially because he knew we talked during all his breaks, before he slept, and on his way to and from work. But I didn't care, I was just angry.

Although we still had our small disagreements throughout the course of our relationship, we still managed to carry on and see each other as much as we possibly could and, of course, kiss as much as we possibly could. Even though we never had many chances to be in an enclosed area alone, we still made it happen when we could.

A few summers passed, and I was almost in my last lap of high school. I had already had my very first job through a program called Tropicana, summer jobs for youth. My relationship was going the same. I remember my father and Tee had a conflict, and she moved out of the house, leaving my brother, Daddy, and me. We hated that she left us. Tee became somewhat like the mother of the house. She was the one who cooked our dinners if daddy didn't, and that was always expected of her. But due to the conflict, she had moved out. My father was still being physically, verbally, and mentally abusive when he got drunk.

He also had it out with me many times, telling me that I betrayed him because I still talked to Tee after she disrespected him. I had to go through that for a long while, but I had Daniel to comfort me. I often told him about some of the stuff that I was dealing with. When I say comfort, I mean so much that I took the risk of sneaking him into my room when my father was not there or when he was asleep. Daniel would sleep on the floor beside my bed for fear that my father would open my door and see him. He even slept in my closet at times. Sometimes he would be in the closet for so long, we would text each other, because my father just wouldn't go out or go to sleep like we had planned he would. Yup, we did take those kinds of risks, just so he could be beside me.

After Tee left, I became the designated cook and cleaner of the house. It was a huge responsibility. I had to do it, though, or I would be cussed out. My family all over the world would hear about how I couldn't cook or that I was nasty. This is actually very far from the truth. Months had gone by while Damion and I were still adjusting to Tee's absence. The only thing that excited me about her absence was the fact that I now had my own room, but that was not enough excitement to not miss her presence in the house. She was really missed.

Remember, I was so in love at such a young age—thinking I knew what love was—so much so that I agreed with Daniel to go visit him at his house. He lived in the West, and I lived in the East, so I had to take the subway all the way from Kennedy to Kipling (the very first to the very last station) to get to his house. It was my very first time visiting after we'd been together for so long.

I cannot recall where I told my father I was going, but all I knew was that I was going to his house, obviously not with the intentions of having sex, but I had a feeling he just would not let this opportunity pass him by. On the whole hour and a couple minutes train ride, most of what I thought about was what my pops would do if he found out that I went all the way to the West on the train alone. However, another part of me was thinking, *What the hell is Daniel thinking about right now?*

I got off the train and followed the bus route instructions Daniel had given me, and I ended up in the same building my older cousin who brought him over lived in. When he came downstairs to get me from the lobby, I asked him if he knew my cousin lived in the building, and he said, "Yeah, his door is right across from mine."

I wanted to pee my pants on the spot. I exclaimed, "Hell, no! You did not tell me! What the hell are you thinking? What if someone sees me?"

Daniel calmly replied, "You're fine, no one will see you."

I took his reassurance and headed up to his apartment. We ordered food, stole occasional kisses, and talked until the food arrived. We ate, stole occasional kisses again, played around, until we finally ended up kissing non-stop while eliminating bits and pieces of our garments. When we were finally naked, I was so nervous when I heard the condom wrapper open, I squealed under his arms. He started kissing my neck, earlobe, and then my breasts. I had never been naked in front of a man in my whole life, so this was scary to me. He started asking me if I really wanted to do this, and so many things were going through my mind. I let out a little squeal again, which he took as a yes, and then he continued with his exploration of my fully naked body. I twisted and turned in all directions, when he finally stopped touching me and said, "I have been waiting so long for this…so very long, but you seem like you don't want to do it, and I will not force you."

I didn't answer. All I wanted to do was cover my body, which felt too exposed. We laid there until we fell asleep. After a few minutes of dozing off, we were up again and kissing and touching. His fingers brushed past my underwear, and it was soaking wet. He started taking them off me and rubbing the area in a slow but very intimate motion, while he kissed every part of my body.

I think I was so intoxicated by the foreplay that I had no idea what was happening. Next thing I knew, his penis was in a condom going towards my vagina, and I closed my eyes. After a long time of trying, he finally got some of it in, although it was very difficult, while still caressing the top half of my body and trying to get me to not scream. Tears were falling from my eyes as he eased his way in.

After a few tries, he made a loud grunt, then cussed, and fell on top of me. I pushed him off and rushed to the washroom where I saw blood between my legs. I started to cuss, scream, hit him, and stomp all over his apartment. I remember it felt like fire between my legs, and I ran out in the hallways of the building, crying and yelling, "Oh, my god! What did you just make me do?" He ran behind me with a towel and brought me back inside.

I was devastated for days after this episode. He tried to comfort me as much as he possibly could, but I wasn't having it. Finally, I had to grasp the reality that it had already happened, and there was nothing I could do about it now. After ignoring his calls or giving him attitude on the phone, I finally accepted it and was ready to move forward with him.

We carried on our relationship for a few weeks, until I noticed he started getting more controlling, like he would require me to call him as soon as I got home from school. Anywhere I went, he would want to know why and how long I would be and who I would be going with. It got so serious to the point where I would be in the mall with my friends, and he would call and get upset if I was there too long. We talked and argued about him getting so controlling, and each time he would say he wouldn't do it again. It would happen again. Foolishly, in love at the time, I would always forgive him.

A few months later, he decided to move out to the east end of the city to be closer to me. His father lived in the East, too, so he had a ride with his father to go to work. Everything ran smoothly where he and I were concerned…for a few weeks of him living closer to me. He still wanted me to constantly visit him after school, or he would come by the house with my cousin and hang out with my brother and my cousin more often. I mean, don't get me wrong, I liked having him closer and seeing him around me, but at times I just felt claustrophobic.

With the constant arguments, we would either be closer or further apart, depending on whether or not I was wrong in the event of an argument. One day, Daniel was walking me to the bus stop when his phone rang, and he started speed walking in front of me and talking low. I asked him who he was talking to, and he said it was a friend. I found out later on that it was his ex-girlfriend, and she was now pregnant for him.

I was defeated, torn, and devastated. I didn't know what to do or how to feel. I cried. I cussed. I screamed for weeks, and he cried and apologized, while trying to explain himself and how it was an accident when she came to pick up her stuff from his house a few months ago. I didn't believe him. I couldn't believe him. All I did was walk away and hope that he would one day say it was all just a joke. However, he never did say that, and she was indeed pregnant. Although I was not sure if the baby was his, for some reason, my gut told me it was his, and I told him not to bother getting a DNA test. That I felt it was his.

We argued countless times after that, and we knew the relationship was going downhill. Somehow, I found the strength to still hang on to our relationship. I mean, I didn't forgive him, but I just couldn't leave. I couldn't see myself without him; he was a part of me now. I knew it was stupid of me to stay, but I guess people do stupid things in the name of love.

When I look back at it now, I wonder what the hell I was thinking to believe that I could still be with a man who had two children at such a young age. I was obviously not thinking! Weeks after weeks were passing by, and some way, somehow, we always ended up arguing about the same thing. No matter what he did or how much he tried to control my every move, the baby still ended up being the topic of our arguments, especially with this news hitting us right after he took my virginity. I always used to say that maybe if I hadn't done it, it probably would've been easier for me to leave. I guess now we'll never know.

My pops now had a woman whom he seemed to be serious about. Other than the one consistent woman he had since we came here, he seemed somewhat serious about this one. I remember the first time he introduced her to us. I was cooking some good old-fashioned bully beef and rice for Damion and myself, when I noticed that he and his lady friend were on the balcony. He called me over and introduced us. She said her name was Christie, but everyone calls her Beno. She was a short, dark-skinned, medium-build lady. I noticed that, although she was a black woman, she did not look or sound Jamaican. I later found out that she was Dominican, and she had three children—an older son and daughter, who were both now on their own, plus a younger son who lived with her at the moment.

Beno and my dad got along really well. Apparently, they had been talking to each other for a while leading up to us meeting her that night. She then started visiting our house more frequently with her son, and then they both started sleeping over.

Although my pops had other women before her that I assumed were still around every now and again, he seemed to have had a different care for her and, like me, a love for her son. We got close and had a good relationship, so much so that I even introduced her to Daniel after she promised not to tell my father about him. She met him and ended up really liking him, thankfully, so we had no conflict there.

Months went by, and I taught her how to cook Jamaican food. She started giving us a taste of multiple Dominican dishes. She started speaking out to our pops about the physical abuse and how it wasn't fair to us for him to hit us for no reason, because we were good kids. My father would reply by yelling at her and telling her not to tell him how to raise his children, because he didn't tell her how to raise hers. They would have these kinds of small conflicts, and then they were quickly back together, again.

One night, I went out to an art function with Beno and Zane, her son, whom I had fallen in love with and treated like he was my own little brother. I even spoiled him ever since that day. I don't know why, but I just had a love for the kid the first time I saw him. He was a smart, loving, caring, short, little, chubby man. As we were on our way back, Beno said she had been calling my pops, but he wasn't picking up. I had a bad feeling about that, but I kept my cool. As we arrived at our building, I noticed before anyone else that his car was parked outside along with the other woman, whom we called "Ms. Consistent."

I started calling him, and he finally picked up. Before I could get a word in, he said, "Rudy, mek me call yuh back, mia leff the building now." (*Translation: Rudy, let me call you back, I'm leaving the building right now.*)

I said, "Daddy, where exactly are you? Because I'm pulling up to the back of the building right now."

He responded, *"Likkle girl, yuh deaf? Mi soon call yuh back."* (*Translation: Little girl, are you deaf? I will call you back soon.*)

After realizing that he was about to exit the building with Ms. Consistent, I said, "Daddy, you figget say a mi and Beno go out? She inna di car wid me now, and we deh beside yuh car!" (*Translation: Did you forget I went out with Beno? She is with me right now, and we are right beside your car!*)

He yelled in frustration. "Shit! Yuh deh a di back now? Just bring har gah di front!" (*Translation: Are you at the back right now? Bring her to the front!*)

It was too late for that. Beno was next to me, looking at me angrily, while my father walked out of the building with Ms. Consistent. Beno was very angry. She just left with her son, and my dad left with Ms. Consistent. Beno stayed mad at us for days. She didn't take my calls or his. Then, one day, I saw her back at the house. Now, I don't know how my pops got himself out of that pickle, but he did. They were back to normal in a week.

With no signs of Ms. Consistent around, one day, Beno asked Damion and me if we would want to move in with her, and how we think our pops would feel if she asked him. We said yes! We would love to, but we had no idea of his thoughts. We were happy with the offer, but we knew we had to try and convince him to do it. Not only because of his past experiences with living with women, but also because he's a very prideful man who tries to do everything on his own. The house we would be moving into was being built, so we had some time to convince him.

We knew what Pops would say, "Mek mi tell uno diss, mi nuh love no woman eno, mi only love mi kids dem, han mi nuh want nuh woman fi run mi or tell mi how fi live mi life." (*Translation: Let me tell you guys something, I don't love any woman. I only love my children. Therefore, I don't want any woman to think she owns me or runs the way I live my life.*) I stilled tried to convince him, especially knowing that this would be more freedom for us, and we would also not have to be afraid to speak.

My pops finally decided to accept moving in with Beno and Zane. The house was about done, and within months, we finally moved in. The house was a nice semi-detached house in a new area on Lawrence Avenue East and Manse Road. Beno did an excellent job on the décor and paintings. It had a modern open concept kitchen and living room with an island to separate the two. The living room had brown three-piece couches, a fireplace and huge flat screen TV. Upstairs had a washroom and three bedrooms. The middle was mine, to the left was Damion and Zane's, and to the right was Beno and my pops'. It had an unfinished basement, a garage, a driveway, and a nice-sized backyard. Although not the biggest house, this was closer to the house that I had imagined when coming to Canada.

We settled in the new house for a few months, and Daniel and I were still going through the motions. With the baby already born, he now had to obviously deal with the mother, and I had to pretend like I was over the whole thing. It still managed to drive me crazy. Especially one day when I called him, and he was rushing off the phone and just didn't sound like his normal self, so I went to his house because I felt like something was up.

When I got to the house, something was definitely up. I opened the door and saw the mother of his child in his room on his laptop, as if she was well comfortable. It made me furious, but I managed to keep my cool and ask her where he was. She simply pointed straight to the shower. That made me more upset. I started wondering if they had just had sex or something. Why was he in the shower? I banged on the bathroom door and told him to get out.

He was so shocked that he asked me about a million times, "What are you doing here?" Then he said, "I have nothing to hide. She knows you and I are together. She just came by to pick up money for the baby!"

I obviously started getting upset and asked, "Why are you in the shower then? Did you just have sex with her?"

"No. I was just showering so that I could go to the bank and get her the money," he said.

I drew a million and one conclusions that day, until he said, "Let's talk outside."

I agreed, but then she came outside too, as if she was his bodyguard. I hissed at her, "Stay out of it!"

She started acting crazy. Then he said to me, "Maybe you should leave."

I got so upset. "Why don't you tell her to leave? Are you crazy?" Eventually, I left and turned off my phone. *How did I manage to end up with a man who is a cheater just like my father?* I wondered.

He called about two hundred times that day alone, not to mention the other days I was avoiding him. My incoming text messages overflowed and my voicemail was full. Finally, I answered after he started to call my brother looking for me. Once again, we argued daily. The arguments started to cool down after we decided to "try and make it work." A few weeks later, Daniel got the news that his workplace was laying people off for a while, and he ended up being one of those people. This is when I did what some people may call the stupidest thing ever, again at such young age. He was receiving unemployment benefits, and those weren't enough to pay his rent and sustain him. So, I spent almost all the money I saved during those times on him. I did everything, including buy him clothes, food, underwear, and more. Not because I had to, but because that is just who I was. I knew if it was me who fell into a situation like that he would have helped me or given me as much money as I needed. I had no problem with doing what I thought he would have done for me if the situation was reversed. This still didn't give him enough reason to stop being controlling and stop thinking that I was cheating on him. Now, there are always going to be men trying to talk to me, and there is nothing I can do about that—something he failed to realize.

One day, I was walking to his house when a cute, light-skinned redhead driving a Range Rover tried to stop me. He honked his horn several times, and I ignored him. He even went as far as making a u-turn and following me all the way to Daniel's driveway. Daniel happened to walk right out of the house when the car pulled up and the guy was about to get out and talk to me. He gave him a furious look, and the guy turned around and drove off. I got cussed out and was told that I was on the road "looking for man," as if I was the one with the baby momma drama. These were the types of things I had to deal with, on top of my father still being an alcoholic and subjected to lashing out at any time.

As the relationship continued, he became more paranoid. I don't know what caused him to be this way; maybe it was the fact that I stayed with him through all of this, and he couldn't believe that I did. Either that, or he knew my worth and didn't want another man to have me. Either way, the more paranoid he became, the more feelings I lost for him.

There was this new Jamaican guy at my school, and we called him a "freshie." I knew he liked me, but I never paid any attention, although I was still cool with him. One day, he decided that he was going to come down to my area and play ball, and he asked me to come outside. I did, just because he was funny as hell, and he reminded me so much of Jamaica. Just as I was about to go outside, Daniel called me. While we were on the phone the freshie yelled out my name from outside my house, and Daniel heard him because my window was facing our driveway. Daniel's tone grew furious. He asked me who it was, and I told him it was just a friend. He started arguing, and I was not in the mood to argue with him, so I hung up the phone and turned it off.

As I walked outside, Freshie was on a bicycle, and we went to the soccer field. There was no one there yet, so we were about to just turn back when I saw a cab pull up by the soccer field. Yup, you guessed it, Daniel jumped out of the cab and started walking towards us. I was tired of all of his nonsense, so I told him to leave me alone. He walked over to me and grabbed onto my right hand.

"I want to talk to you…and now!" he demanded.

"No, let me go!" I said.

Before I knew it, Freshie grabbed onto my left hand, and Daniel started cussing at him. Freshie cussed back, all while they were both holding onto my hands. I don't even know how I couldn't move. They were both stronger than I was, and I was too stunned to do anything.

Daniel yelled, "Eediot! Let go off my woman! She don't want yuh!"

Freshie snorted, "Yuh nuh see a you she nuh want? Stap act like a waste man, and let har guh." (*Translation: Can't you see it is you whom she does not want? Stop acting like a fool and let her go.*)

"Yow, a matta fact, stay outta dis, cause yuh nuh know how far we a come fram!" (*Translation: As a matter of fact, stay out of this, because you have no idea how far we are coming from!*)

Freshie grabbed me around the waist fully and attempted to walk off. "Mi nuh care how far uno a come fram, just low di girl and gwaan." (*Translation: I don't care how far you guys are coming from, just leave her alone and go.*)

Daniel walked up behind us and demanded one last time, "Yo, Rudy, tell him fi gweh nuh, and come mek mi talk to yuh." (*Translation: Rudy, tell him to go, I need to talk to you.*)

To my surprise, Freshie pulled me in and planted a kiss on my cheek and said to Daniel, "Waste man, talk to dat. Yuh nuh see the girl nuh want yuh?" (*Translation: Fool, talk to that. Can't you see the girl doesn't want you?*)

After that, all I remember seeing was Freshie being flipped off the bike in a complete three hundred and sixty degrees and falling right onto his side. Blood started gushing from his arm. They punched it out for a couple seconds, until Freshie jumped back onto the bike and rode towards my house. Daniel ran behind him and slipped and fell in the middle of the road. I just walked behind both of them. I was so astonished. I never dreamed of the day I would see two men fighting over me. I just didn't know what to do. Again, I was so young!

When I finally got to my door, Freshie was covered in blood and was trying to knock down my door. Daniel charged towards him, trying to show him a text on his phone in an attempt to prove to Freshie that I actually wanted Daniel and not him.

Zane opened the door, and Freshie asked to see his mom. When I walked right by him and closed the door, they were still yelling and screaming at each other.

Freshie told him, "I don't care about any texts!" But still Daniel insisted.

After a while, it quieted down and then Beno came home from work and ran into Daniel. He was still outside, angry as hell. She somehow talked him into leaving before my father got there. I told her and Damion what happened, and to be honest, we laughed it off for a bit. Then the calls and texts started rolling in again from Daniel. He even left a few voicemails, one sounded like he was crying, the other like he was crying in the shower, in the other he threatened to call my father and tell him everything, and so on. Of course, I answered his calls after I heard that one. We talked that night till morning. He didn't want me to hang up because he was afraid I was going to call Freshie right after. He begged me to come see him the next day so that we could talk.

   I went, just so I could tell him that I was seriously over the relationship and that I just couldn't deal with it anymore. He was still convinced that I was ending it because of Freshie. I wasn't, because I gave Freshie a piece of my mind that day too, not only about that surprise kiss to act like we had something going on, but also, why the hell would he go to my house and knock down my door? What if my pops was home?

   Daniel still didn't understand that I was just over it. He begged, pleaded, and cried, but I was no fool now. I knew that if I forgave him again like all the other times, he would go back to being his old controlling, paranoid self. Although I knew it wouldn't be easy for my heart, I just had to do it. I left him crying. I just couldn't take it anymore.

   When I got home later on that day, my father called me downstairs and started cussing at me, trying to hit me, saying that he heard from the neighbours that I had two men fighting over me at the door. He cussed and asked me if that was why he brought me to Canada, if it was to let men fight over me, and that he has never seen this in all his life living in Canada. The cussing went on and on for days, and of course, my family all over the world heard about it.

   Summer was rolling in, and I was still not talking to Daniel. I did pick up his calls every now and again, just to see how he was doing. I guess he didn't realize that I was serious, until he asked me to come over, and I told him no, because we were not together. He started threatening to call my father, again. I thought he was bluffing, so I told him I didn't care if he did it and hung up on him.

   As I was getting ready to go out to a cultural boat cruise downtown with Beno and her friends that night, all I heard my father say on the phone was, "Why are you calling me now, because things are not going good? Why didn't you call me before?" My heart sunk, although I liked my father's reply, I couldn't believe he actually called. Then I got more nervous when my father called me outside in front of Beno's friends and gave me a slap in my face. I couldn't even concentrate properly after the slap. He started cussing and grabbing me, and Beno ran out and told him to let go of me. He told me to go to my bed and that I couldn't go anywhere but right back to Jamaica.

That night I cried so much. I've never cried that much in my life. There were so many built up emotions that I wanted to kill Daniel. He knew how my father would react. How could he do that to me? I had no answer to that question, but I did what I had to do and changed my number. I didn't want to hear from him ever again.

I was also mad because I knew my father was not going to be able to send me back to Jamaica. It would be the first time I'd ever rebel against him, because I knew I would not go on that plane. It would take an army to get me to go on, because my pops alone would not be able to do it. Everyone, even Beno and my cousin who liked Daniel very much, was mad at him after he did that. He called down the house phone trying to apologize, neither I nor anyone else in the house showed compassion towards him.

I guess some would say that Daniel had been coming from a place of pain and hurt, but looking back, he drove me away. I knew I shouldn't and didn't want to continue to live my life like that. I made a lot of what I would call 'avoidable mistakes' with him, only because he was my first, and I thought he would have been my last.

This goes back to what I mentioned earlier. One often models or tries to model the adult figures around them while growing up. For me, that figure was predominantly my big sister, Tammy. Ever since I knew her, she stuck with the father of her child for over eleven years. I never saw her with another man in a relationship.

Lesson:

Know yourself and your worth. The minute you start to accept less than you deserve, that's going to be the only thing people offer you, until your requirements are higher.

Invest in yourself. Do things that are good for your mind, body, and soul. Meditate and eat things that feed your organs. This way you learn to fall in love with yourself before falling in love with anyone else and end up losing yourself.

9 Discovering My Passion

Life was getting back in order now that Daniel was gone, and I started applying myself more as an individual. I had already fast-tracked through high school. Therefore, at this point, I was pretty much done with high school.

I was still working at my second retail job in a shoe store that I loved. The staff and the manager, Manny, who was an understanding and kind-hearted white man, were the people I was close to at the time. My first retail position, working in a call centre, where I was selling credit protection to people in the United States, was my worst job experience to date. I started working with that company not knowing what to expect; I just needed a job. When I started there, I was told the hours would be an hour after school until 11:30pm. I was sending myself to school at the time and I needed the money. I had no idea I would've been forced to sell these things. I had supervisors breathing down my neck pretty much telling me to force the clients to buy this product that most of them had no interest in buying.

All I remember hearing all day long was, "Rebuttal, rebuttal, rebuttal! Guys, remember, if you don't make any sales I will send you home." With that being said, I worked my butt off so that I wouldn't be sent home. Until one day, I had a ton of homework. I tried to do some on my break that night. When I realized it was freezing rain outside and I would have to go home on the bus, and then that long walk to my house, which meant I wouldn't get home until about 1:00am, I asked my supervisor if I could leave early, and she said, "No."

So I called my pops, who I was sure was not doing anything that night, to ask for a ride and he said, "I didn't send you to work so find your way home!"

After explaining to him that it was freezing rain and I had nothing to put over my head for the walk, he still said, "Nope."

That night, I started on my way home, and as I was walking, I was cold and wet. I just stopped and started crying. A million things were going through my mind, like how could he be so selfish, especially when he was no longer giving me money for school and I had to fend for myself. Couldn't he just appreciate that I was ambitious? Those thoughts were replaced with anger. By the time I got back to the house, I saw him in the garage just chilling, drinking, and smoking. I was furious. I went back to work the next day and stayed until the Friday of that week. Then I quit and got the job at Si Vous Play Scarborough, the shoe store.

Around these times, I was spending a lot of time working on "Healin' Scars," the non-profit organization that I started with a friend of mine, Ubaid Mojadidi, a university student at the time that was in love with and devoted to fashion as much as I was to working in my community with the young people.

I spent a significant number of hours creating administrative infrastructure, building stakeholder networks, and developing programming materials. I knew I wanted to impact change in the young people in my community, and I was convinced that by running my own organization that would be possible.

A previous teacher's assistant, Halgan, whom I had met a few years before and stayed in contact with, helped with the developing of the mission and vision statements as well as the one pager that we planned to present to potential partners in the community. I didn't know where I would house this fully fleshed out organization, so I emailed a man who came to my school and did a presentation, after which we stayed in contact as well. His name is Eman. He was under thirty years old and had just started running a three million dollar funded non-profit organization. We met that same day at his office, and he said he would provide us with the office space, rent-free, and access to the resources there.

We accepted the offer and got to work immediately. Within a few weeks, we had auditions for our very first fundraiser talent fashion show. The auditions and planning processes were hectic and more difficult than I anticipated. We endured a lot of issues with getting the proper flyers out and to our target population. It was also very difficult to get designers in the city who were willing to be involved. Most were just egotistical and thought they were better than a small organization that had just started.

Through this process, we managed to build and maintain relationships with multiple known organizations and people within the city. Regardless of how difficult this process was, it always brought me back to why we started in the first place. When the young people would showcase their talents as if it was all that mattered to them in this world, no matter what they might have been going through, they would always have a shining smile on their faces.

Although the space we used for auditioning was very tiny, we managed to make it work and got through all the interested talents—singers, rappers, artists, graphic designers, actors, dancers, photographers, and clothing lines. Our days seemed short and our nights seemed long. I will never forget the late nights closing up the office after auditions and waiting out in the winter cold for the bus. We never complained. As a matter of fact, until now, we never noticed it because we were so passionate about it.

The big day was approaching. We had help from all the staff and associates from Eman's organization supporting the event. Plus tickets were going faster than I thought. Everyone who was a part of the show had to sell tickets, and all four vendors paid for their spot at the event. The sleepless nights and the tiring days were coming to an end. The day was finally here, and I must say, leading up to this day if I did not have Ubaid by my side, I probably would not have survived this whole thing. It was so much work!

As I showered, I thought, *Well, man, this is it. This is the big night where everyone will learn about the organization I started and my reason for believing in healing through the arts.* My phone was ringing off the hook. People who had tickets on hold and people whose tickets were bought for them by those who just wanted to donate to the cause were all calling. I had forgotten to pay the final payment for the venue, so I had to rush there to pay it.

I had two outfits for the night. Along with all the performers, I met an amazing host—Jelly Too Fly, a Toronto rapper, whom I met at the Remix Project (a Toronto arts-based organization) graduation. Greeting the guests upon arrival were Jasmine, my volunteer assistant at the time, and my closest friend to date, Jemelia. The clothing line vendors were all in position. The early birds were checking them out and making their respective purchases before taking their seats. As soon as the crowd was seated, everyone settled in and the show began, everything ran smoothly and according to plan, straight to the very end. It was certainly one of the most amazing nights of my life. I actually shed a tear while delivering my thank you speech. Everyone enjoyed themselves and left with kind words and well wishes for the future of my journey.

The day was long gone, weeks had passed, and the young women's program continued. Although we lost money from the event, I never made it a big deal. I just knew I had to make a better financial plan in the future. I moved on to being the chair of the board at Eman's organization while running Healin' Scars and still working part-time at Si Vous Play. It was then that I got a call from Ubaid, one day, asking me to meet up.

During our meeting, he expressed that being a part of the organization would be too much for him while he was in school and doing his personal work in the fashion industry, so he parted from it. We remained close friends after that, although that meeting left a bitter taste in my mouth. I left it at that. I mean, how could I ever be ungrateful or burn a bridge? Leading up to that point, Ubaid had played a vital role in the organization as well as in my life. At the time, he gave his all to that event, and it could not have happened without him.

However, moving along, I managed to run programs successfully with the revenue from the event for about two to three months, and then the money ran out. I refused to apply for government funding at the time, because I just did not want to be restricted on how to run my own program.

Time was flying by, and before I knew it, I was growing closer and closer to Eman. He was not only my mentor, we were now close friends. Together, we attended executive meetings, community meetings, and kickbacks together. I was sort of like his right-hand person. Out of the office, we were a tag team...or so I thought.

Summer was approaching, and I was meeting new people. I watched myself become a better me. I sort of liked the flow now. Fewer arguments with Pops, because I was hardly home, and he even took a small trip to Jamaica at one point. Summer was finally here, and I got a job at Tropicana, again. This time my job was not as a program participant but as a program coordinator.

This was some serious stuff for me. I just couldn't act like it was any old job; this was *the* job! Because I was a program participant years before, and a young person with passion, it was natural to hope to become the coordinator, and my dream was finally coming true. I was on a three panel interview, and the process was not easy at all. It was super intense. I spent a lot of time preparing for the position. But let me tell you the story leading up to the job. Being the chair of the board at a reputable organization, you meet a lot of cool people who know a lot of people, and through networking you get first dibs on hearing about new jobs, and you also get good references if they see potential in you.

I was a paid advisor and mentor for a youth council in Scarborough, and one day I was invited to one of their strategic planning meetings that included trustees, funders, and other key stakeholders. I knew then that I wanted to work for the council. These folks were astonished by my presentations and the way I carried myself, so much so that one of the ladies who saw me around and apparently heard about me approached me. She happened to be not only the trustee representative but also a director at Tropicana. She immediately began to tell me about the position that was open for a program coordinator. I told her I would definitely like to apply and asked her how I should go about getting started. She said that I should just send her an email and she would take care of the details.

Before I knew it, my application process was over, and I got a call for an interview. During my first panel interview, I was a nervous wreck. I was shaking and sweating under the table. A few days passed after the interview, I was convinced that I didn't get the job. I thought maybe I just wasn't good enough. Then, I finally got a call from one of the ladies on the panel. She said that my application was late, and they would love to offer me a coordinator position. However, in the time being, they were full with that position but wanted to offer me a job as administrator at one of their other offices.

I was a little bummed out, but I talked to God for a few seconds and humbly accepted the position. I was going to start about two weeks later, so I started preparing myself and telling everyone that I got the job. When I got to the office on the first day, I had my own desk, phone, and even a special chair. I thought for a second that maybe I could be content with this. But knowing me, I obviously was not.

Days had passed, and I just felt like I wasn't doing enough, like my skills weren't being applied enough. I started applying for part-time jobs when I got home. Even then, I still felt like I was not being useful enough at Tropicana, especially when I noticed that in the office there was someone in a coordinator position whom I just knew I could do a better job than. I didn't bother complaining about that person. I just took the initiative and started doing program coordinator duties. I started interviewing participants, calling employers, and scheduling on top of my administrative duties. Before I knew it, everyone in the office saw my potential and started treating me like a coordinator.

One day, my team leader decided to let me do the training for the program participants along with another coordinator, Melissa James. We met up at the head office ready to train the young people. Before that, we'd never had any conversation other than casual office talk. However, it was amazing how much we clicked throughout the training that lasted about a week or two; we were excellent together. I thought to myself, *Wow! This girl is the business!*

We worked well together, and I even realized that I started picking up skills from her to add to my existing ones. We became friends, and it was then that I knew we would probably be friends forever. We had conversations that I had never had before. She always challenged my way of thinking, and I always challenged hers as well. Nonetheless, if we had a disagreement, it never left a bitter taste in our mouths. We always agreed to disagree and moved forward without an itch or scratch.

After doing the trainings, the director called me one day to ask me how the job was going and said that an office in the west end may need my help if I would be willing to travel. I told her I had no problem doing so, and it was then that I got the official title as a Program Coordinator and the salary to match. I went from a decent $13.00 per hour to a swooping $17.00 per hour. At that time, minimum wage was about $10.00 per hour, which was what most, if not all of the people that I went to school with were earning. I was doing pretty decent for myself.

You know what they say, "More money, more problems." And, you guessed it, the expenses started rolling in. I started sending money to my family in Jamaica on a bi-weekly basis. Plus I started contributing to the bills in the house. I still had a little something left to purchase my necessities or save some small change here and there after all the external expenses. Things were going alright. Other than a little work politics, all was well.

Summer was now approaching its end. My pops was on his way back from Jamaica, and I was still rolling around with Eman like a big shot. When my pops arrived, I was not home, but I saw him the next day. That was after Beno started complaining about him and some antics he was up to in the garage. My pops was a man who chased Remy Martin with Heineken on a daily basis and smoked cigarettes and weed like it was nobody's business. So imagine the type of man my pops was. If it did not benefit him, or if it wasn't about his job or children, there was a ninety-nine percent chance he did not care.

Apparently, Beno saw some inappropriate photos of him in the garage with some people as well as some from Jamaica. She was furious, and when he came to the house the following evening, she gave him a piece of her mind. My pops is a man who hates to be talked down to or made to feel less than a man, so he decided to move out. The argument got crazy, and he just left. He took his stuff and left us. The last thing I heard him say was, "My kids already chose you over me, so if you guys think you can pay the bills without me, I will see how well you all do it alone."

Lesson:

Find your passion or something that makes you experience your highest peak of happiness, and do just that. Always remember to volunteer in the career of your choice. As much as you may think you like it, it is important to really get familiar with its ins and outs as much as you can. And if you still want to do it after that, then you know you genuinely love it, so work hard and kill it!

Mental Illness, Suicide & Depression 10

The weeks were coming and going by quickly. My contract ended, and we were heading into Christmas. The energy in the house was bittersweet. Pops was gone, and we were kind of happy. Beno was sad that the bills were piling up. Although she claimed he didn't contribute much, the little that he did contribute was missed, and she was feeling lonely. I could see it in her eyes. She seemed sleepless, but I didn't ask for much information that was not given to me voluntarily.

I, on the other hand, immediately panicked when I realized that my savings was running out. I couldn't seem to find a job immediately and, for some reason, I thought no matter what happened he should have never left us. We were his and, technically, Beno was a stranger who was not obligated to keep her ex's children living with her after a breakup.

Christmas was creeping up on us, and Damion was barely working. I contributed whatever I could towards the bills, but that never seemed to be enough. I was so hard on myself. I stopped eating and socializing, and I was reluctant to answer my phone when it rang. It was then that I knew I was going into depression. It was like falling into a hole. I was conscious that I was falling, but I just didn't know how to get myself out. That is the best analogy I can use to describe how I felt at the time.

I locked myself in my room for hours, days, weeks, probably even months. I barely ate, and if I did eat, it would be late at night when no one was up in the house. I blamed myself for his departure. I kept having flashbacks of all the times he beat me, and I always made sure my room was pitch dark, because I did not feel like I deserved sunlight.

The depression, however, got worse, and I started to consider suicide. I mean, like full-out suicide. I had multiple scenarios made up in my head daily of how it would happen and what would be the fastest and easiest way to die. However, along with those thoughts, I'd still beat myself up by asking myself things like, *How can you make this happen to you? Why are you even allowing these thoughts, Tasheka? Just hang in there, things will get better.* I had to give myself pep talks when it was getting too serious. I had no one to talk to. I just didn't think anyone would understand, especially Jamaicans. I thought maybe they would think I was going mad.

There were times I felt so weak and dried out, my body could hardly get out of the bed, so I would just force myself to go back to sleep. Sleeping was my escape. I loved to sleep. I thought maybe if I slept enough the pain I felt would not be for a full day. Most of the day, I would be emotionless.

I don't know what triggered the depression, but everything just felt like it was crumbling. It felt as if the world was closing in on me, and I had no way of escaping. I tried to get out whenever I could. No one could tell by looking at me that I was going through such deep depression and mental illness. I kept a smile and joyful face whenever I was outside of my room. I laughed and joked so much sometimes I even overdid it. I just didn't want anyone to ever feel sad or alone. I knew the feeling; it was not a nice one. I had gone through it for a long period of time, and I would never wish that feeling on my worst enemy. Therefore, I vowed to always leave people better than I found them and never take anything for face value. You never know what battles people are fighting behind closed doors. However, when I got back inside my room, I was back in deep, again. I couldn't stop my mind from straying, no matter how hard I tried.

One day I was downstairs in the kitchen peeling an orange and, out of nowhere, I decided to bring the knife up to my room. The act of taking the knife with me was subconscious. In the room with the knife, I fell asleep. Hours went by, and I still hadn't left my room. I over-thought and over-analyzed everything. Then, finally, I reached for the knife that had been there for about a day and a half. I started carving on my skin. I was so focused on cutting it that I was no longer over-thinking. Then I caught myself. It was then that I knew this was a serious case. I started researching depression and mental illnesses. Without delay, I self-diagnosed myself and realized I needed to get out of this. This place was dark; it was not a place for me, I knew I could do better.

I started reaching out to teachers and small organizations that had youth programs and let them know I was open to doing motivational speaking, especially to programs that dealt with mental health. I started receiving bookings and referrals. That kept me on my feet and out of the house. I engaged with young people who might have gone through or were going through depression. I tried to identify with them by letting them know that it is not a nice place to be in. My advice was to hang in there and seek help, because no pain lasts forever.

I am not saying it will be easy, but it is worth it to get out and seek help. I was just too prideful to do so, but I knew if I had I would have gotten out of that state sooner than I did.

After every speaking engagement, I would change up my power point presentation, making it more detailed by including resources and more information on how to get help. When I look back, I realize that as much as I was doing the motivational speeches and workshops around these issues, I was not completely recovered. When night fell and I was all alone in my bed, it was a struggle to keep myself from not slipping right back into that depression. I fought my way out as much as I possibly could, and I never let it take me that far, again. That was a difficult time in my life and, when I remember it, I count my blessings. It could have been worse, but instead I used it as a stepping stone to help others. My experiences have touched many lives.

One of the main reasons for this book is to show that not everything that sparkles is gold. Everyone is going through something, it may not be the same as what you are going through, but they are going through theirs nonetheless. Therefore, one should never be quick to pass judgment. Hang in there. Weeping may endure for a night, but joy comes in the morning.

A few weeks passed, and I was doing pretty well. My nights were getting better, and I spent time with colleagues, speaking at colleges and universities, and talking to my friend on the phone at night. These became coping mechanisms, especially the burying myself in work part. Until one day, I met an older man who claimed he knew my father. We started talking, joking around, and then we exchanged numbers. When he called me one day, he said he wanted to see me to talk about something. I wouldn't hide anything from Beno, so I told her that I would be meeting up with him at the front of our house that day, and she said, "Okay."

I met up with him, and to this day, I cannot believe what he asked me. He said if I let him perform oral sex on me, he would give me anything I wanted. I was so startled by the request. I asked him if I would have to do it back to him or if I would need to do anything else. He assured me that all he wanted to do was that, and I would just have to sit back, relax, and enjoy it.

I said to him, "Are you joking right now? Why me of all the women in the world? Why me?"

He said, "Nothing too complicated. I see that you are a trying girl, and you are a go-getter. But now it looks like you are struggling, and I could help you. The only catch is that you allow me to do this to you."

I could not believe my ears. I told him I would think about it and get back to him. Now, to be honest, I did consider the offer. I went and did thorough research on this man, and nothing came up fishy. I learned that he had a decent life, worked two jobs, was a widower, and had a really nice house. He definitely had some money in his possession. I was like, *Damn, what should I do?* I did as any other girl would do; I called my best friend, Kokoman.

At the time, my best friend was an Egyptian and Sudanese guy I met in high school. He was much older than me and was in his fifth year when I started high school. We met through a mutual friend, and we became close—as close as I was with the guys in my community back in Jamaica—so close that I started hanging out with him and all his other friends, too. They always looked out for me like a little sister, and I looked out for them just the same.

So I told Kokoman about the offer I had just received, and he said, "It sounds legit. You should try it out one time and see. Since you are legally an adult now and have never had that done, you could use the help."

I was still nervous and scared after our talk, so I did the second best thing—I told Beno and my brother about it. Damion didn't have much to say at first, but Beno was fifty-fifty. I thought to myself that night, *Man, this could be my opportunity to have a better life. I can just let him do it and then save up the money. But then would this not be like prostitution?* I had so many unanswered questions, so I marinated on it for a few days. One thing I came up with for sure was that if I did not take the opportunity I would always wonder what would have happened if I did, and I decided I did not want to carry that burden forever. So judge me if you want, but I did not let the offer pass me by.

I felt like a big shot, acting older than I was, as usual. Speaking of older, we never spoke about our ages. He didn't know mine, and I didn't know his. I don't think I would have wanted to know. So I called him up and gave him a time to pick me up. When he arrived, after texting my friend his license plate number, I hopped in his nice, expensive looking car. I immediately started to observe the interior during our awkward small talk. To my surprise, his car was clean, organized, and smelled very good. I was impressed.

We went to a very nice hotel, and as he checked us in the room, I was a nervous wreck, but I tried to act cool. We entered an amazing hotel room. He told me to take whatever I wanted from the mini-fridge and then headed straight to the shower. I thought to myself, *Is this guy serious? He thinks I am just going to act all normal and have a field day in this place?* I just sat there quietly until he returned from the shower. He had his shirt on and a towel around his waist.

I never really looked at him much before. I realized that this man had a beer belly, a stiff one just like my pops. It was then that I wanted to run out of that room and act as if we'd never met. But I gave myself a mental pep talk. I couldn't leave now, I was too far in, and I probably would never have forgiven myself for leaving.

After a little small talk about our expectations of each other, he had a beer and, apparently, he was ready. I must say it took us about an hour and a half to finally get it to really happen because I was jumping and moving all over the place. Once it was done and over with I almost disliked myself. I had no explanation why I did. I just did, and that was that. I felt nasty. He was not nasty or anything. I just felt dirty or perhaps just disappointed in myself. Although I was relieved he didn't try anything funny, he just did what he said he wanted to do.

He suggested we stay the night, but I said no, I wanted to go home. I went home, and I showered at least three times before leaving the bathroom. I called my best friend and told him what happened. He always had a way of making me feel better about things. Then I went straight to bed. The following weeks were not much of what I expected, but were nevertheless appreciated. I was given gifts, was brought or sent lunch at least three times a week, and sometimes even dinner. When family members had the opportunity, they took full advantage of the free food part of the situation. Before I knew it, the offer of the gifts started to become more and more expensive, and I started refusing them.

I can remember vividly that one day he offered to buy me a car and I said, "No, thank you. I do not want anything from you that I will not be able to purchase or maintain by myself without you."

To which he responded, "You have too much pride, and that is not going to take you very far in life."

It was then that I started to dislike him. That statement altered my whole perspective of him. We argued continuously after that. I must say, however, he was a decent man when it came to respecting my boundaries.

One day, I woke up to three private missed calls. When I finally caught the fourth one, all I heard was, "You B**ch! Leave my man alone! He doesn't want you… blah, blah, blah…" I swear to you, I immediately burst into laughter. I honestly couldn't believe this. I didn't know what to do but mute my phone and laugh. When she finished her rant, I hung up the phone.

I am not one to disrespect my elders. No matter what or who you are, I will not disrespect you. I will try my very best to just avoid the situation. It was obvious this woman was older than me, and I had no business arguing back with her, especially with the use of foul language. So I did the next best thing to do in that situation, I told Beno that she called. When I told Beno about the call, she laughed too, not at the situation at hand, but rather the behaviour of an adult. After we enjoyed a good laugh about it, she told me to call him and make sure it was his people and not one of my friends playing a trick on me.

I called him, and I was bombarded with the use of all manner of foul language and disrespect geared towards me once again from the same voice I woke up to that morning. I couldn't help but laugh, again. I really don't know why, but I just found it funny. She cussed for a very long time until she was finally fed up of me not answering her, so she hung up.

At that point I thought, *Well, wow, man, I gotta just let this one go now, this is it.* He didn't even tell me he had a woman. All I knew was that his previous wife had died, so as you would imagine, I was obviously surprised by the phone calls. Not only that, but I would now have to change my number, which is super annoying, considering that was the number on my business cards.

Don't forget that I was still living in my stepmother's house without my father. Therefore, I was not absolutely content. I tried to come up with all possible scenarios of how I could get out before she told me to leave. It was only natural for me to be thinking that way. Which stepmother would still want her ex's children to be living with her forever and bring back continuous memories of him?

Now, I do remember expressing to this man in a previous conversation that one of my goals was to move out of my stepmother's place before it was too late. A few days after the outrageous phone calls, I came home to a couch set and a centre table in the garage. I will not lie and say I did not expect some sort of gift, because I did, especially when I was no longer answering his phone calls. For all I knew, it could be her calling again. I immediately called him and told him to come and get his stuff.

He said, "No, it's yours for whenever you're ready to move out." He then promised me that he wouldn't buy me anything else against my will if I would just answer my phone and let him explain. He obviously had no logical explanation as to why this woman was calling me other than he was sleeping and she took his phone. He said he was sorry.

I was like, "Yeah, yeah, whatever..." knowing in my head that things would never be the same. I just wanted him to think I was cool. Everything obviously went downhill afterwards. This was an easy decision for me to make, considering I was never comfortable with the situation in the first place.

Every time I think back to that day in the hotel, I have a disgusted feeling towards myself. But life happens, and you have to live with the choices you've made. I was trying my hardest to not be too hard on myself, but every time, even to this day, when I think back on the whole thing it's like I just want to beat myself up. For allowing myself to let a man older than me, whom I barely cared for, see a sacred part of my body, for letting people convince me to continue taking stuff from him—as if I don't have a mind of my own, right?—for my father leaving us. Not that I blame him for my actions, it's just that I think if he was around like he should've been I would not have let a man like that come close to me, especially come to my door. Knowing the type of person my father is, he probably would have killed us both. Most importantly, why was he not taking care of his children like my friends' parents were doing for them? All I'm saying is if he was being a father as he should've been, I wouldn't have had a need for any "help" from this man. I should have been able to call on my father whenever things got tough and I needed help, not being around a man whose mouth wanted to have a field day between my legs in exchange for some "help." When my father filed for us to live with him, he had promised to support us for our first ten years in Canada; he didn't even do it for half of that.

Anyway, by now this man and I had not communicated in a while. I was still doing whatever it was to survive. I tried to keep myself from falling back into a deep depression, while keeping in mind that I may have to move out of this lady's house soon.

Speaking of my father and moving out, one day Beno and I got into an argument. I can't quite remember what the nature of the argument was, but it was nothing too serious. Anyway, she started to cuss, and I walked out of the house away from the argument, just to take a breath and calm myself down. I called my best friend, and we talked and laughed for a bit. When I got back to the house, to my surprise I walked right into my father. I greeted him and then headed straight to my room. Moments later, I heard banging on my door. It was my father, cussing me, telling me I was disrespecting Beno in her own house, and if I can't have respect then I should leave…blah, blah, blah.

My father has a strong demeanor, and he can be very intimidating. I don't know where I got the strength and courage from that day, but I started cussing and talking back to my father. All I can remember saying is, "You have no right to be coming here cussing me. I pay my own bills here. I'm not living for free, and you do not do anything for me. You are the reason for my ongoing depression and suicide considerations. I can give you a million reasons why you have no right to be yelling and screaming at me for no reason, especially over a simple situation between me and the person you said I put over you."

He was so shocked and surprised at everything I said, his only reaction was, "Mi nuh care, I wud be better hoff if yuh dead. Rudy, weh mi do fi mek yuh want commit suicide, ee, likkle girl? All mi do a bring uno come here and do the best weh mi can do fi take care a uno, and uno diss mi!" (*Translation: I don't care. I would be better off if you were dead. Rudy, what did I do to make you want to commit suicide, huh, little girl? All I did was bring you guys to Canada and do the best I could do to take care of you, and all of you dissed me!*) He went on and on, until he finally left the house.

I play this day over and over in my head all the time; it was the only chance I had to say a little bit of what had been bothering me for years. It was not all I wanted to say, but it was good enough for the moment. I instantly broke down after he said he would be better off if I was dead. I couldn't say anything more. I guess this was a part of the healing process, but I'm positive I was more broken than I was healed. Come to think of it, at the time, I didn't even have energy to think about why Beno would call him in the first place. I was so caught up in saying what I wanted to say that it didn't even occur to me that she actually called him. In fact, I doubt I would have even cared considering I was so taken aback by his response. "You would be better off if I was dead? What have I ever done to you other than try to please you all my life?" That was it for me. I wrote him off after that day. I wouldn't even wish death on my worst enemy. How could my own father wish death on me? What did I ever do to him?

It was so crazy that Beno herself couldn't believe he said it. She immediately turned to him and told him he was wrong for that one, but he didn't care. He walked right out of the house without another word. I was so hurt, I couldn't stand to bear the pain, but I knew I didn't want to go back to that dark place of depression, again. I had to fight it. Even though I slipped in and out because it was not an easy battle, in the end, I can say today that I won the war.

Life went on, and I must say that during all this, I had some great family and colleagues that supported me through it all. Most, if not all of them, had no idea I was going through this, but they played a very instrumental role in my journey by just being positive and supportive people who gave off positive energy whenever I was in contact with them, especially my closest friends, Kokoman and Jemelia, my good friends, Priscilla, Antonio, Jody, Melissa, Akilah, Alisa (Tekk-Tekk), and a few others. I appreciate you all more than you will ever know. All the laughter and joy you brought to my life when I needed it, especially during those times when my mood changes were severely unpredictable, from being either really high or super low. Thank you.

Lesson:

~ Everyone you know is fighting their own battles. And ninety-nine percent of the time, the way they react to you has absolutely nothing to do with you and everything to do with them and their personal battles.

Those with mental health depression or suicidal consideration always remember, "The universe took its time on you, crafted you precisely so you could offer the world something distinct from everyone else. So whenever you doubt the importance of your existence, you doubt the God energy that is greater than us both."

-By Rupikaur and revised by Tasheka M.

When You Think It's Peace & Safety, There Can Be Sudden Destructions. But I Am a HUSTLA!

11

You ever heard the Jamaican saying that goes, "Trouble neva set like rain." (Trouble never sets like rain)? Meaning, when the sky gets cloudy, you can tell it is about to rain. However, unlike a rain warning, there are no caution signs for troubles.

Life continued. I attempted to build relationships with professionals who could help me with my mental illness. I still facilitated programs while job hunting, and still struggled to keep my head above waters, like most people in this country. At this particular period of time, I was spending a lot of time out of town. I figured I could be more productive out of my comfort zone, where I was subjected to relapse. After the weekend, I came home to a letter from Beno telling Damion and me that in the next three months we would have to move out, because she did not want to lose her house, and the little money we were giving her was not enough to contribute to her maintaining her mortgage and bills. Therefore, she would be renting the rooms to students so she could keep her house.

She obviously said the part about loving us, how she wished she did not have to do this, and that she wished us all the best…blah, blah, blah. I called Damion immediately and asked him if he got the letter. He said that he had and that I should meet him on our street on my way back inside. Then I went straight for a walk. A few minutes later, I met him on our street, and we dissected the letter, paragraph by paragraph, to get a full understanding of what she was saying and, most importantly, what we were going to do. We talked for a bit, and I pretty much said I could always go to Jemelia's. Her mom had told me that I would always have a room there. She had two empty rooms in a five-bedroom house, so I knew there was that option for me. But what was my brother going to do? I don't know if the situation were reversed if Damion would have up and left me then and there, but I was not about to leave him. I had to figure something out that would work for both of us.

As soon as I woke up the next morning, I called Eman, Jemelia, and Kokoman and gave them the news. To be honest, they were not surprised, because I had already told them that I knew this was coming eventually. The only question now was where was I heading, and what was going to happen with Damion?

Within a week, I gathered all my resources and all the money I had. I called a few of my colleagues, and they advised me to apply for Toronto Community Housing for Damion and myself. I knew well that the waiting process for these types of things can be brutally long—I knew people who waited anywhere from two to ten years for these things. Therefore, it was a long shot, but I got down to business the minute I knew I would be qualified for the opportunity and wrote an emergency letter, visited all the necessary offices that helped with the application, and got the ball rolling.

Before I forget, I would like to say a special thank you to Flo and S. Brown at Tropicana Community Services who supported me one hundred percent through this process.

Now, I was born a hustler. I just think it's a part of my DNA. It pretty much follows me everywhere I go, from ever since I had to visit my mom's friends to get lunch money back in Jamaica. I had two godfathers, who in my opinion were the wisest hustlers I knew—Mikey Slu and Coppa. From that to coming here and having to sell weed for my pops, I just had a hustling style engraved in me. This just triggered me to activate the *hustla* in me. I made a few calls and started purchasing clothes, shoes, accessories, and all things stylish. I even had a few people credit me the stuff because they trusted me. I filled a suitcase with the items and began to sell. I sold from sun up to sun down, to past and present co-workers, family members, friends, friends of friends, you name it, I sold to them. After a month or two, I paid back those I owed and then started doing my own thing. I saw an opportunity to send these items to Jamaica and make more money, so I started packing boxes and sending to Jamaica for a few friends of mine who were out of work and had no access to my mother to sell for me.

Trust me, if they had access to my mother and she knew they were selling for me, she would take as much as she could from them, as any mother in her position would, ha ha. All of this was happening in secret. No one, except those immediately involved in my operation, knew about it, and I liked it that way. However, I realized at one point I was losing money because I was paying to send the items to Jamaica, but I did not raise their values to match the shipping costs. Plus the costs to transfer the profits back to me from Jamaica were sometimes high.

These became little setbacks for me, because I still had to pay the folks who were working for me back in Jamaica. If you know me, you know I made sure they were paid before I paid myself, because I was afraid of embarrassment and unfairness, and I stayed true to that fact. Also, keep in mind that I was still responsible for supporting my mother, from time to time. This was also another expense for me. As I settled into the selling of clothes stuff, I realized the profit was not much, and my suppliers weren't always reliable. Therefore, it was not worth all the time and effort I was putting into it, while not getting much in return. Then and there, I knew I had to find another way as time was running out for me to move out of the house. Behind the scenes, I was still applying for jobs and applying myself as a community worker, nonetheless.

Until one day I got a call from Eman that he had a job for me. It was a part-time community based researcher position in Jane and Finch. However, I would still have to travel to other hoods (at-risk communities) and facilitate workshops with multiple groups of young people. I was game. It was a job, and I needed one, even though the journey from my house to the office was about two hours by bus. I took it anyway. However, this job was not to start until another month or so. Therefore, I was still stuck trying to find a way to make money, considering that this was going to be a part-time position and I still had bills and expenses. So, of course, I did the only thing I knew how to do almost as good as social work. I started selling weed. Of course, it was not as easy as one, two, three, but I had my connections. I knew a guy who was a huge supplier of the herb. The only thing now was to gain his trust, because I was about to ask him to credit me his marijuana.

But before I did that, I had to first find my customers. I am not talking about the small stuff my pops had me doing. I am talking about being a supplier to someone like my pops. That meant selling by the pound not dimes, twenties, and half-a-quarter bags. I did not want the weed in my hands longer than a couple hours when I got it. I just wanted to get rid of it and make back my money as quickly as possible, so I knew I had to sell it by the pound. I called the man, and we scheduled a meet up.

We met, and I showed him the little money that I had left in my name. I told him my plan and that I already lined up my customers. Lastly, I tried my best to make him feel comfortable by telling him all the top men's names that I knew he knew. You know what they say, it's not what you know, it's who you know. Afterwards, I patiently waited for my call back.

As you read this, you may think, *Then Tasheka, why didn't you just go get a minimum wage job?* Well, my answer to you is when you are as young as I was and on your own with as many expenses as I had, a family in Jamaica that depends on you, and you are pretty much homeless, wouldn't you do what you know how to do? One thing I knew for sure was how to be a hustler, and as an individual, I always tell myself I do not want to ever go backwards. Meaning, I paid my dues, I worked the minimum wage jobs and volunteered a whole lot, and all that jazz already. Besides, I had no plans of doing this thing for long. I wanted to save up enough so I could survive when I eventually moved out, just because I knew it would be more difficult than it already was. So, I say this again, judge me if you must, but I just did what worked for me at the time.

For the younglings who are reading this, especially the ones who have been a part of programs that I coordinated or facilitated, this is not a pass for you to do something like this. I'm writing this so you understand that it is not an easy road or an easy life for anyone. You may have seen me as your leader and never thought I'd done these kinds of things, but trust me I've seen and done a lot and am continuing to see plenty more. So, be wise and don't be a fool. My granny always says, "Puss and dog nuh have the same luck." (*Translation: Everyone's luck is different.*) You may see someone else do something and get away with it, but that doesn't mean you won't or can't get caught.

Apparently, this was not enough problems for me to deal with. One afternoon, I came home again from out of town, this time from Brampton City. It was Damion's birthday, and he was having a couple of friends over for food and drinks. He asked me to cook some rice and peas for him, so I came to help him out with that. I was not even in the house for fifteen minutes before Beno came in with an angry face, mumbling in her throat. She gave no greeting whatsoever, then she picked up the TV remote and turned down the music Damion was playing. She proceeded to walk back towards the coat closet, when Damion came up the stairs and said, "Weh, yuh tun dung di music fah? Yuh nuh si mia listen to it?" (*Translation: Why did you turn down the music? Can't you see I am listening to it?*)

I replied, "Yuh si mi tun dung nuttn? A she come in and a mumble an tun it dung. Mi cah wait fi come out a di people dem place." (*Translation: Did you see me turn down anything? It was she who walked in mumbling and then turned it down. I can't wait to get out of this house.*)

I did not even finish my statement fully, when all I heard was, "Get the f**k out! Don't wait, go now!" she cussed and swore at the top of her voice.

Without answering her, I left the kitchen, walked up to my room, took the bag I had already packed, and took a walk. As I was walking, I called Jemelia and told her what was going on. She knew I was mad and frustrated, so all she said was, "Are you on your way to my house or do you want me to come get you?"

I told her I was about to hop on a bus coming towards her. As she hung up, the phone almost rang immediately. Beno called me, and all I heard was, "Listen to me. Do not come back to my house. The only reason you should come back here is if you are coming to get your stuff."

I replied "Okay!" and hung up.

When I arrived at Jemelia's house, I told her mother what had happened at the house, and she said I could stay there and pay whatever it is I could until I got back on my feet.

I can vividly recall what I said to her when she presented the offer. My exact statement was, "Thanks, Ma, but I only need three months here, and then I will be out."

She and Jemelia displayed signs of confusion on their faces simultaneously. Now, as close as Jemelia was to me, she had no idea I had mental health and depression issues. The room she offered me was in the basement, and I knew if I stayed in the basement I could fall right back into depression. I solved that issue by leaving my belongings downstairs and sleeping upstairs beside Jemelia or in the prayer room. The second issue was that I knew this was Canada, and just like Beno, it only takes time before someone with whom you are staying either gets tired of you or disagreements change the relationship. This family meant too much to me for me to jeopardize our relationship, so I knew I had to come up with a game plan if the subsidized housing thing didn't come through in time.

The following day an ex-associate of mine and I went in the pouring rain for my stuff. We made about three trips before it was all cleared up. While I was packing and struggling in the rain, Beno sat in the living room and said nothing to me. On my last trip, something happened that broke my heart. Zane came to me in the room with the saddest eyes I've ever seen from him and asked me if I was really leaving him. I sat him down and explained to him what was going on and why I was leaving. I gave him all means and ways of contacting me and told him I was his big sister, no matter what, and that I would always be there for him for whatever he needed.

His last words to me while he helped me put the last few garbage bags in the car were, "Rudy, I won't have no discipline or guidance when you are gone. You know that, right?"

I could not answer him. I felt like crap for leaving him. My heart sunk. It was then that I thought maybe I should have fought to stay with him a little while longer. But what needed to happen then was already happening, and there was nothing I could do about it anymore.

It wasn't that I was surprised by her actions; it's just that I didn't understand why she couldn't just ask me to leave. It seemed to me that was what she wanted all along. Why would she make something so small seem like a big issue? But then again, what may have been small to me didn't necessarily mean it was small to her. Maybe she felt disrespected by me saying I couldn't wait to leave, which was just me speaking the truth, considering the energy in the house dropped drastically after she gave us the letter. Although I stayed mad at her for a while, when I look back at the situation from a more mature and empathetic perspective, it was evident she had her own personal issues, most of which I actually had nothing to do with, but I somehow got caught in the crossfire. That is just human nature, and it happens. After a while though, we talked over the situation and moved forward from it, and to this day, we still have a mother-daughter relationship. I love her to pieces.

While staying with Jemelia, I still had not heard back from the weed man, and that might have been a good thing. I was now staying with Jemelia's mom, and she is a Christian woman. My conscience would not have allowed me to do a thing like that in her house. I, myself, am a very spiritual person. I practice meditation. I pray each and every day, and that is probably the only thing that continues to keep me going. Therefore, I had to respect her home.

I was there for about two weeks, and would you believe me if I told you that none of my siblings called me to see where I was or what was going on with me? Yep, none of them did, until later on that week Tee called and asked me where I was.

I said to her, "Look how long it has been since I left the house and neither of you thought to call or check on me! It's now you want to call?"

She answered with an attitude, "Oh, obviously, I was busy and I know you must be good. So, are you going to tell me where you are?"

I said, "No, but I'll be fine, thanks for asking. Bye." I then hung up the phone. I was not in the mood to deal with that at all. If something had happened to me, all those days had passed before she decided to call, and she would have been sorry.

Anyway, I applied for three colleges that same week. I thought it would make sense, considering I was only working part-time. Obviously, the universe had other plans. I applied and got accepted. When filling out my student loan application, I learned that I could not go any further without my mother's and my father's income information. To cut a long story short, I had access to neither. I called the offices for days trying to explain my situation. They refused, even when I said I might be able to get my mother's but not my father's. They said they needed both. I was broken. I felt defeated. Everything I tried had failed. Nothing was working out. I prayed day and night, asking, "God, why me? Did I not try hard enough? What more do I need to do?"

Then, one day, Jemelia saw that I was sad and asked what the issue was. In the midst of telling her, I broke down in tears. She held me close and said that I was not being the Tasheka she knew and that I was never one to give up or accept defeat.

I hadn't cried like that in all those years with all the things I was going through. However, at that point, my cup just felt like it was overflowing. I don't know if God put Jemelia in my life for a specific reason, but whatever that reason was, I will forever be grateful, no matter what.

That night, as I broke down, she knew this was not something I would normally do. I was always a soldier, and I faced my problems head on. At this moment, though, I just couldn't take it anymore. I saw the confusion in her eyes. She cared so much, but she just didn't know what to do. I picked back up my pride and did not allow the tears to last any longer. We talked as she continued to hold me. She was there for me in a way that no one has ever been before. It was almost as if she felt my pain, as if it was her own.

I am usually the person who feels other people's pain and gives my last to others, so to be on the other side of the situation and have someone give to me selflessly was a blessing. To this day, I adore her more than she will ever know. I've done things for people who will never be able to repay me, I have contributed to the changed lives of many, and I have done things for people who will never do anything for me. Jemelia is probably the one person who I can genuinely say is the most consistent person in my life and who has done things for me that I just don't think I will ever be able to repay her for.

I've had people who have known me since birth and have never seen me cry or seen me in a vulnerable position. It is very difficult for me to let people so deep into my life, and I am proud to say that I have no regrets letting Jemelia into my life the way I did. I swallowed my pride and accepted help when she offered. Not very many people can say I've done that with them, and that is something I am currently working on—just being able to accept help from others, especially when I need it.

I was pretty much homeless, although I was grateful to have a roof over my head. I was pretty much broke. My mother still depended on me, and now I was not able to attend school like everyone else my age. To me, this all meant that for the rest of my life I was going to have to work twice as hard if I wanted to succeed like the others with one or two parental or guardian's support and/or a degree. I currently read and research as much as I can just to know as much as I can. I am a committed life learner and always open to new knowledge. Therefore, I am equipped to face the world of those with a formal or informal education.

A quick message for the folks in a single-parent household, don't be jealous of those with two parents. You never know their story or what they are going through. Don't envy a soul for what you know nothing about. And for those with two parents, don't envy those that live on their own. It may look peachy, but it could also be their worst nightmare. In both circumstances, I know you may feel sometimes that your parents are annoying or too over-bearing, but hang in there with them. They only want the best for you. I know sometimes their approach may not be the best one. It can sometimes seem nagging, annoying, and even unfair, but oftentimes, they just don't know better and need you to just sit and talk to them. Don't be afraid to speak and work on issues together.

Parents, open up your ears more to your children. They need you more than they need anyone else, and fear does not allow them to want to open up to you. Stop bringing up the past! If you have already scolded or spoken to them about the issue, do not bring it back up every chance you get. Stop telling your friends and other family members about how bad or unacceptable your children are. This builds up resentment towards you that you may never know about. Finally, support your children in whatever it is they desire, even if it is not what you were used to when you were young. Never forget this is a different generation. Things and times are changing. Try to research it before you criticize it, learn more about whatever it is before you shut it down. Young people need you more than ever; it all begins at home. And never forget that some people develop quicker than others do. Therefore, take your time and work with your child where they are.

Talk, talk, talk! I cannot stress communication enough. No matter what the situation is, say what you are feeling, understand that it is okay to feel, but it is more important that you make what you are feeling clear. In whatever you do, always remember that no one can read your mind. As a result, never assume they know. You owe it to yourself to let them know how you feel.

Anyway, I continued to deal with life as it came. I worked this part-time job, travelling to and from work at the Jane and Finch office location. One day, I ran into an old friend of mine. He and I started to link up on the phone and talk on a regular basis. Finally, he invited me over to his house. I went to his house, and for a man under thirty years old, he was ballin'! Let me tell you, this man lived in the most exquisite condominium I had ever stepped foot in. Everything was modern and luxurious. I was flabbergasted.

I kept asking him what he did for a living and how he afforded all of it. I knew he had a legitimate job, but there had to be something else to him. We sat down, ordered some food, and started reasoning. He told me that at one point when he lost his job he was sending females to Jamaica to smuggle drugs inside their vaginas. The business was doing okay. He saved up all his profits and made investments. Then, luckily, he got a job in his field and then he stopped doing it.

I was like, "Wow! That's crazy! Thank God you didn't get caught!"

We continued to eat, laugh, and talk about the past. Then I told him what I was going through at the time, and he asked me if he could bring me somewhere to show me something, and I agreed.

We got into the car, and about thirty minutes into the drive, I stopped seeing the city. All I saw were trees and roads. I was a bit paranoid and wondered where the hell this man was taking me. *I haven't known this man in a while; maybe I shouldn't trust him this much with my life.*

Subsequently, following my thoughts, we were finally approaching houses, some very big houses. We pulled up to a brown and black one with two BMW's and a Honda Civic parked in the driveway. He didn't knock. He used his key to open the door. We entered. The house looked decent, like a regular home, when we entered, not as exquisite as his condominium, but decent for those with a normal life.

There were voices coming from the basement of the house. We walked towards the sound, until we got to the basement level of the house. I think it is safe to say that what I walked into was the most drugs and money I had ever seen in my life. I was shocked, to say the least. He saw the look of surprise on my face and said to me, "You are a soldier, and that's why I brought you here to show you this. Don't get cold feet on me now."

I responded, "Nah man, mi good."

He showed me the whole operation, introduced me to all the folks, and pointed out who was in charge of what. To my utmost surprise, there was a young white lady in the house. She did not look more than twenty-two years old, and she apparently was one of the big bosses in the business. I really thought it had to be some sort of joke. I keenly observed everything she did, how skillful and tactical she was. She was cooking at one point, then at another she was wrapping and bagging parcels.

He explained that he was no longer a part of the team, but they were his friends, and he checked in on them every so often. He also said they were all professionals, and most of them had decent jobs. However, this life was an enhancement to some and an addiction for others.

Afterwards, we all went upstairs, conversed, and ate, then the girl asked me if I wanted to make some money.

I said, "No, thank you. This is not my style."

She rolled her eyes at me. "What are you talking about? I would never ask someone like you to smuggle anything. I'm no fool."

After remembering that my friend had said most of them were professionals, I said, "Oh, I just thought that maybe that is what your offer would have been, but anyway, what do you suggest?"

She smiled and said calmly, "If you have any girls who want to work, send them to me, and I will give you $1000 for each girl. As long as they are willing to work, your money is a guarantee."

You remember how I said my face was in shock a few moments before. Yeah, well, after she said that, my face was covered with a smile. I couldn't believe what I was hearing! I mean, I already had girls in mind that would be down. I told her I was game. We agreed that she would email transfer me the money as soon as she met up with one of the potentials. What happened after that was not my business.

On the way home, I thanked my homeboy for bringing me, and he gave me a lecture that all I needed to do was clear my debts and save a little money, and then I was out. I agreed.

He dropped me off at home, and I went to bed with all the girls on my mind who would be down. I just couldn't wait to wake up the next morning and call them.

Morning finally arrived, and I made a few phone calls. So far, I had one who was one hundred percent in. I sent her to meet up with one of the members of the team, and my money was sent to me within minutes. An extra two hundred dollars for being so quick, I already loved it. I sent the whole two hundred dollars to my mother, and then I called the phone company to pay off what I owed. I had one outstanding personal phone bill as well as a cable and internet bill that I took over at the house when my father left. I put down a payment on both of those. I gave Jemelia's mom a small change, and then I was back on the phone connecting with potential girls.

After my third girl, I had already made about $4,500, and I quit. I was out. I couldn't do it anymore. For two reasons: one, I was the person doing motivational speaking, youth working, and all that jazz, telling young people to stay away from that kind of lifestyle, but yet I was sending young women to risk their lives for $3,000 or so per trip. I was disgusted with myself. I felt like the biggest hypocrite ever. Two, I am a God-fearing person, currently staying in a Christian home and going to church on a consistent basis, so all of it just didn't feel right.

I managed to pay off most of my bills. I was able to lend a friend $1,000, which I never got back, and I was able to send my mother whatever I could when I could. All that money slipped right through my fingers as soon as it came to my hand. I fasted and I prayed after I quit, but for some reason, up to this day, I still feel like crap when I think back at making such a mistake.

Now, my three months were almost up. I was about two months in, and I still hadn't heard from the housing people yet. I was worried sick, so I took matters into my own hands. I started calling and emailing everyone I knew that was connected to the housing corporation and told them what was going on. They told me I was accepted onto the priority list and to just sit tight and wait it out for a few more months.

I said, "Nope, can't do! I already promised myself three months and not a day more."

I made a few more calls, did what I had to do, prayed, and waited for it all to fall into place. On my birthday, January 3, less than a month later, I got a call from a housing corporation representative saying that there was a two-bedroom apartment available for me to go look at. I was actually pulling up to the driveway in my friend's car. I called Jemelia immediately after the lady hung up and told her to come with me and let's go look at it.

We went to the apartment and looked inside. I was nervous as hell, considering it was in the "hood." I thought maybe it would look old and trashy. When we entered the apartment, the floors were nasty and torn up, I didn't like it. I asked the man who seemed to be working in the building if they were going to change it, he said that yes, the apartment floors would be renovated before I moved in.

I was still a little iffy, but thank God I had Jemelia with me to knock some sense into me. I told the lady immediately that I would take it, and I asked when I could sign the lease. She said that I could come sign the lease in about two days, and then in about a week the renovation would be done, and I could move in after that.

I was overjoyed. I would finally have my own place, my own space, and all the privacy in the world. I called Damion and told him to come, because I would be including him in the lease as an occupant of the second room. He was surprised I had gotten it so soon, but he was happy, nonetheless.

Three days later, we met up at the building, gave proof of our income, and signed the lease. On our way out, new information was brought to my attention. Damion told me he had a child on the way. Although this news was exciting for me, Damion seemed to fear the idea. I never stressed the issue. I thought maybe this was a normal feeling at that stage of the situation. Nevertheless, nine months later, I was blessed with my very first beautiful niece, Jayda Desire Jones-Mason.

About a week later, I was scheduled to pick up my keys and pay the first month's rent. I did just that and, within a few days, I moved in. I had nothing except my clothes and two measly blankets in garbage bags and storage bins. Damion was not ready to move in yet, so for the first few months when I moved in I slept on the hard, cold concrete floor on the blanket.

I didn't have much money the first few nights, but I did have thirty dollars, and I used a portion of it to order Chinese food—one order of veggie fried rice and an order of veggie noodles. I ate some and stored the rest in the fridge, until the next day. I had an oven pan, so I put another portion in the oven, heated it up, and then ate, drank water, and went to work. I did this every day until the Chinese food was finished.

Luckily, I got paid that week. It was difficult, but I had to do it anyway. All I cared about was that I had a place I could call my own. I was feeling too much pain from sleeping on the floor, and my pay was not enough to purchase a bed, so I called the rent-to-own store and took out a bedroom set. The bedroom set arrived the following day, and I was happy to have a bed. My place was empty, but I had a bed, a place to rest my head that was my very own, and I felt at peace.

Lesson:

~ *Never give up. The best view is revealed after the hardest climb. You may fall off here and there, but never give up. It's okay to get your head back in the game after setbacks.*

Setbacks are like track and field training hurdle bars, if you didn't go over the first time, take a few steps back and charge at it again. Even if you buck your toe on your way over, always remember that you still passed that stage. Just never stop trying!

Open Letters to Mommy & Daddy

Dear Mommy,

I am writing this letter to get some of the positives and negatives of our relationship off my chest. First, I will start with the positives, and no, I do not love Daddy more than you! ☺

I cannot credit only you with all of who I am today, because that would just be unfair to the other women who were mother figures in my life for a significant amount of time in your absence, like Tammy, Beno, and Denise. However, I want to let you know that the greatest gift my father could ever give me was you, the soil in which he planted the seed of me.

I remember when I was young, whenever you came home from work, you tried to spoil me the best way you could, and I will never forget that. Those were some of the happiest days of my life. Even though we were poor, you tried your very best to make sure we weren't lacking in anything. You loved me unconditionally, as any mother would their child.

There are not enough words in the universe to describe the love I have for you. Mommy, you are a phenomenal woman. One of the most important things I learned from you is that tears are not equal to weakness, because I have seen you cry because of our poor conditions, but you are the strongest woman I know.

I want to let you know that I am sorry that your mother never gave you the love you gave me. I know you always tell the stories of how she abandoned you and did not send you to school, but sent her other children, which resulted in you not being formally educated, though street wise. Thank you for never giving up on life because of what your family did to you. Thank you for always forgiving them, over and over again.

Although these were your motherly duties, I still want to thank you for being my personal nurse, doctor, chef, life teacher, and more. I am utterly grateful for your hard core; each disciplinary scold was out of pure love and therefore was very effective. Many live their lives wondering if their parents really love, accept, and value them, but with you, that was never the case. I was always sure of you.

Now to the not so positives. Mommy, you will never know how difficult it was for me to have to be the daughter of a mother who smokes weed. I mean, none of my friends at school's mothers ever smoked weed. I know you never meant for it to be that way, but I just want to let you know it was a difficult time for me.

Another difficult time for me was the simple fact that you were never the one at my PTA meetings or any school events. It was always Tammy, and while I love having a cool big sister who supports me—I don't want to seem ungrateful—but it would have been good if you could have been there sometimes, too. However, when I think of the circumstances surrounding why you weren't there, I always have to stop myself from being selfish. I hate to say it, but I told you so. I told you I never liked my baby sister's father, but no, you still wanted to try with him. You see, now it didn't work out. Although I am sorry that you had to go through that, I am not sorry that you left him. He contributed to many unhappy times in my life, and I am glad you are happy with who you are with now.

Although I know you did this for my betterment I want to let you know that I resented your decision to send me to Canada when I started going through all that I did. I mean, there were days and nights that I wished I had a mommy to be there with and for me, but you were not.

I also want to let you know that I used to run in the dark at night whenever you sent me to go and beg people for lunch money. I was just ashamed of it, and sometimes I didn't even go, and then I came back and told you that they weren't home. For that, I am sorry.

I would like to end this letter off on a positive note with hopes that you take this into consideration and accept my confessions and apologies. I want to let you know that I will never dislike you for your constant miserable nagging and love for money, ha ha, because I know at the end of the day, if there is one person in this world who prays for me morning, noon, and night, it is you.

Therefore, with all of me and more, Mommy, I want to say thank you for being you and doing all that you could, when you could, and how you could. I love you with every fibre of my being.

A special thanks to Tammy, Beno, and Denise for being mothers to me when Mommy was not there.

Yours truly,

Bashy, Bammy, Artyy, Tasheka

Dear Daddy,

I am writing this letter to get some of the positives and negatives of our relationship off my chest. First, I will start with the positives, and no I do not love Mommy more than you! ☺

Firstly, I must say that I am forever grateful for your existence. I don't think I would be who I am today with another person as my father. You have been more of a father to me than many fathers have been to their children. I want to thank you for taking us to Canada and giving us the opportunity to become something.

I wish that sometimes we could just go back to the days when you lived in Jamaica and I saw you on holidays. You were my best friend, my idol, and the love of my life. Anyone who knew me around those times could tell you how much I adored you. Especially Mommy, who would often say you are my favourite parent. I would brag about you to my classmates and friends.

When you left for Canada, your absence was felt deeply, but I didn't want to show it. As you know, I called you every chance I had just to hear your voice and talk to you; and for that very reason you would tell people that I was your only child that did not call you just for money. I even called you when I first started menstruating, instead of telling my mother who was there with me.

Daddy, as I write this with tears in my eyes, I am saying to you that I needed you around. A lot of times things were not okay, and I needed you. Mommy just could not do what I wanted you to do, and that hurt me so much. When I came to Canada, you were a completely new person, nothing like the fun, understanding man I knew you to be. Daddy, you beat me for no reason, just because you are an addict in denial. That experience scarred me, but it made me who I am today.

Daddy, do you remember when I told you that Cousin Mark tried to come on to me and you did not believe me? You just said that I loved being around big people too much. Well, you were wrong for that, and no matter what, you should have believed me and spoken to him, because if I was a fool at that time, he probably would have taken advantage of me.

I want to let you know that I forgive you. I forgive you for all the things that you have done wrongfully towards me, and I love you unconditionally, but you have to go seek help.

Daddy, I wish you never did some of the things you did to me, because as a man who treats his daughters like that, what do you expect other men to do to us? Many choices that I have made where men are concerned, I could have avoided if you were around.

Although we are all adults now, and you may want to say these things are in the past, no matter what anyone says, I believe the past impacts the future. And for that reason, I want to let you know that I accept the apologies that you did not give to me. I also want to let you know that bragging about me when I was younger hurt my siblings a lot and resulted in grown hatred towards me. For that, I am hoping you take the time out and apologize to them as well.

Yours truly,
Rudy

Healin' Scars

*** On January 18, 2015, I lost a high school mate who travelled to the United States on a scholarship to gain access to paid education and follow her dreams of becoming a basketball player. She was found dead in her dorm at the age of twenty-one, and we still don't know the cause of her death. On December 9, 2015, I lost my dearly beloved grandmother who was one of the kindest and most hardworking women I know. It was during a very critical time in my life that she passed away and her passing was devastating to the family, but thanks to this unfortunate incident, I am now closer with my father than ever before. I am working on healing my scars as well as ensuring that others in similar situations will not have to go through some of the same challenges I faced. Therefore, a portion from the sale of this book will be paid towards a scholarship fund for young people who are ambitious but struggling financially to follow their dreams, or immigrants who have no familial support after high school. Those awarded with this scholarship will get assistance with education costs and living expenses.***

What's Coming Next

Look out for the continuation of the journey and find out what happens next. How I managed to pull through and get some furniture and kitchen supplies in the apartment. Damion finally moves in, then my big sister, Tee, and the father of her unborn son moves in as well.

You will see what happens when I was accepted to the first ever Premier's Council on Youth Opportunities for the Ontario Provincial Government, as well as the beginning of my travels, and the gentleman I met.

Also learn how I attempted to climb the corporate ladder while running a speaking company and being an entrepreneur all under the age of twenty-five and without a university degree.

All this and more will be featured in Part Two of *Resilience*.

Let's Connect!

Now that you have read a part of my story of strength, let's connect. I'd love to hear yours.

Tel: 647-609-6752 or 647-458-2365
Email: BookTasheka@gmail.com or tasheka@tashekamason.com
Facebook: Tasheka R. Mason
Twitter: Ms_Tasheka
Instagram: Ms.Tasheka
Website: www.tashekamason.com

A Message to all RESILIENT WOMEN:

"You became a diamond out of hard life. Understand that you are Magical" – Tasheka

---

Tell YOUR STORY.
Love YOUR STORY
Honour YOUR STORY
Don't be ashamed of YOUR STORY.
Because you've overcome all the hardships in your life to this day and that proves that you cannot be broken.
STRONG WOMAN, YOU ARE MAGIC!
– Tasheka